Challenges Faced by Iraq War Reservists and Their Families

Challenges Faced by Iraq War Reservists and Their Families

A Soul Care Approach for Chaplains and Pastors

KEN J. WALDEN

PICKWICK *Publications* · Eugene, Oregon

CHALLENGES FACED BY IRAQ WAR RESERVISTS AND THEIR FAMILIES
A Soul Care Approach for Chaplains and Pastors

Pickwick Publications
An Imprint of Wipf and Stock Publishers
199 W. 8th Ave., Suite 3
Eugene, OR 97401

www.wipfandstock.com

ISBN 13: 978-1-61097-785-2

Cataloging-in-Publication data:

Walden, Ken J.

Challenges faced by Iraq war reservists and their families : a soul care approach for chaplains and pastors / by Ken J. Walden.

xii + 136 p. ; 23 cm. Includes bibliographical references.

ISBN 13: 978-1-61097-785-2

1. Iraq War—2003–2011—Chaplains. I. Title.

DS79.76 .W34 2012

Manufactured in the U.S.A.

Dedicated to Michelle

Contents

Preface

SEVERAL COUNTRIES AROUND THE globe are engaged in warfare within their domestic boundaries and/or on the international stage. Military conflict can be found all across South America, North Africa, Asia, and Europe. War often impacts military personnel and military families in many similar ways. The United States of America has not been immune to warfare; their military personnel, along with their military families, are presently grappling with war's particular effects.

In this book I examine the emotional, physical, psychiatric, relational, and spiritual challenges experienced by military reservists and their families during pre-deployment, deployment, and post-deployment related to their involvement in the Iraq War. An important aspect of my research is my location relative to the topic: I am an Air Force Chaplain Major Reservist serving since 2000, prior to the Iraq War, and I am also currently pastoring my fourth church since receiving my Master of Divinity degree ten years ago. All of the churches had members who were veterans of various wars. They always appreciated my chaplain reservist role, as they understood the importance of this vocation; I often made it a point to connect with them on our common military ground. A few times a year I wear my Air Force Chaplain uniform to Sunday worship services, and this helps start conversations about military life among the church members.

In this book I investigate two interrelated problems caused by the Iraq War: 1) the unprecedented, multifaceted suffering experienced by U.S. military reservists and their immediate family members, secondary to actual or possible combat deployments to Iraq; and 2) the unanticipated challenges their suffering poses to the military chaplains, civilian pastors, and family members caring for them.

The primary audience for this research is military chaplains and pastors who are in a position to provide care to military reservists and their families, whether before, during, or after service in the Iraq War. The secondary audience includes scholars in the disciplines of practical theology and pastoral care and counseling, as well as other persons interested in supporting military communities. I recommend a soul care approach for chaplains, pastors, and others so they may offer effective support to military reservists and their families negatively impacted by the Iraq War.

My research is focused on a holistic approach to soul care provided by chaplains and pastors relative to emotional, physical, psychiatric, relational, and spiritual problems experienced by U.S. military reservists and their immediate families, whether or not actual or possible combat deployments to Iraq have occurred. While the soul care provided by chaplains is assumed to be interreligious and valuable to nonreligious reservists and their families, when attention is given to the work of pastors, its focus is on Christian communities. Furthermore, although some military families may experience spiritual renewal and positive growth associated with their service in relation to the Iraq War, my research almost exclusively focuses on reservists and families who experience difficulties.

The literature in the fields of both pastoral care and counseling and practical theology is severely limited in its attention to the problems experienced by military reservists engaged in war. Through the use of a practical theological method, my research will contribute a comprehensive analysis and understanding of problems faced by military reservists and their families affected by the Iraq War. Furthermore, the practical theological method will also result in recommendations for a soul care approach for chaplains and pastors to use in support of reservists and their families suffering from their experiences in the Iraq War, and to guide congregations toward participating in such support.

In chapter 1, I introduce the problem being addressed and the structure of the argument; the research questions and methods; and the scope, limitations, and contribution of the project. I also offer an analytical review of the literature that addresses pastoral care and counseling in the context of military life.

Chapter 2 consists of a discussion of military chaplains' roles and experiences during wartime and combat, based on chaplains' first-person accounts of combat and war experiences, military and government publications, and articles in general magazines and newspapers written by chaplains themselves or by reporters interviewing chaplains. These will advance my argument for the necessity to provide soul care for military reservists and their families.

Chapter 3 details the history of the military reserves before the Iraq War, with emphasis on the identity of the reserves as primarily an immobile organization that generally did not enter international war zones.[1] It lays the groundwork for chapter 4, in which changes in the nature of reservists' service will be described.

Chapter 4 describes the demographics of the military reserves, their families, and then examines in detail the difficulties they faced during the Iraq War. Several resources will be used, such as the 2006 Annual Report of the Reserve Forces Policy Board;[2] "U.S. Air Force Reserve Snapshot: A Summary of Facts and Figures about America's Air Force Reserve"[3]; "Managing the Reserve Components as an Operational Force"[4]; and the National Military Family Association.[5]

In response to the difficulties faced by reservists and their families, chapter 5 then describes in detail a soul care approach that will enable chaplains and pastors to offer holistic care to reservists and families negatively impacted by the Iraq War.

1. A publication particularly important to this discussion is Paulson and Krippner, *Haunted by Combat*.

2. The Reserve Forces Policy Board acts through the Assistant Secretary of Defense for Reserve Affairs and is the principal policy advisor to the Secretary of Defense on matters relating to reserve components. See "2006 Annual Report of the Reserve Forces Policy Board," http://www.dod.mil/ra/rfpb/reports.

3. "U.S. Air Force Reserve SNAPSHOT."

4. U.S. Office of the Assistant Secretary of Defense for Reserve Affairs, "Managing the Reserve Components as an Operational Force."

5. National Military Family Association, http://www.nmfa.org/site/PageServer.html.

Chapter 1

Introduction and Discussion of the Core Problem

WHY HAVE I CHOSEN to focus on the Iraq War? The Iraq War techni-
cally lasted for over seven years, from March 20, 2003, to August
31, 2010, but little is known about how it affected military troops, especially reservists, and their families. I have investigated two interrelated
problems: 1) the unprecedented, multifaceted suffering experienced by
United States (U.S.) military reservists and their immediate family members, secondary to actual or possible combat deployments to Iraq, during
and after the war; 2) the unanticipated challenges their suffering poses
to military chaplains and pastors. The holistic approach of soul care is
one means by which military chaplains and civilian pastors (pastors) can
assist reservists and their families who are experiencing a wide range of
problems. Traditionally, each military branch uses a unique term to refer
to those who serve. For example, it is routine to call *soldiers* those who
serve in the U.S. Army, whereas they are *sailors* in the U.S. Navy, *marines*
in the U.S. Marine Corps, *airmen* in the U.S. Air Force, and *guardians*
in the U.S. Coast Guard. For the purpose of simplifying my references
to these various military personnel, "soldiers" refers to military personnel in all branches. Moreover, for the same purpose, "reservists" refers to
members of the U.S. Military Reserves, which consists of the Air Force
Reserves, Air National Guard, Army Reserves, Army National Guard,
Marine Reserves, Navy Reserves, and Coast Guard Reserves. Reservists'
"family members" refers to relatives living in the same household. The

Challenges Faced by Iraq War Reservists and Their Families

Iraq War has taken an unprecedented toll on military reservists and their families across the United States.[1]

A review of our history will remind us that the concept of the citizen-soldier has existed since the earliest history of the country. During the American Revolution, citizens were called upon or volunteered to take up arms against British soldiers or to provide support roles during the war. Later, the organized militias transformed into different organizations, such as the Army reserves, Marine reserves, Navy reserves, and Air Force reserves, among other branches of the military.[2] Similarly, since that period, military chaplains, pastors, and other practitioners have provided a variety of care to support the military. Historically during times of war, military reservists served primarily in expanded roles on U.S. bases for brief periods of time, and not in war zones. However, starting at the beginning of the Iraq War, the level and type of service expected of reservists changed considerably. Following President George W. Bush's Executive Order 13223, signed on September 14, 2001, military reservists can be involuntarily mobilized for as long as 24 consecutive months.[3] Consequently, military reservists' service was uniquely demanding in the Iraq War in several ways: the actuality or possibility of extended and multiple deployments to Iraq; the substantial presence of reservists in Iraq; and reservists' unprecedented combat responsibilities in the war. The service of military reservists has also been financially advantageous for the U.S., a fact confirmed by Lieutenant General Charles Stenner Jr., the Air Force Reserve Command Commander, in the following excerpt from an article published in *Citizen Airman*:

> Reservists save taxpayers money because they are called to active duty in a pay status only when the nation needs them. When they are no longer needed, Reservists return to their civilian lives and a non-pay status. Nearly 80 percent of the Air Force Reserve is maintained on a called-up-as-needed but ready-now status. "We provide nearly 17 percent of the Air Force's capability for about 4 percent of the Air Force's budget," General Stenner said. "Our units and people make outstanding contributions to the national defense."[4]

1. Musheno and Ross, *Deployed*, 152–53.
2. Gross, *Air National Guard*, 1–20.
3. Bush, Executive Order 13223.
4. U.S. Air Force Reserve, "AFR 2012: Command Makes It Easier," 16.

This significant reliance on the reserves has led to unprecedented suffering by reservists and their families. Hundreds of thousands of reservists and their families encountered life-changing experiences during pre-deployment, deployment, and post-deployment. They have suffered a wide range of Iraq War stressors—physical, emotional, relational, psychiatric, and spiritual—that have often resulted in increased rates of chronic and acute physical illnesses, untreated or unmanaged psychological issues, family disturbances, and spiritual and religious challenges. It is important to underscore the fact that such a categorization of problems is not rigid; these dimensions of life are fluid and overlapping. The human experience consists of a series of events, multiple relationships, and varied interpretations that rarely fit in unyielding or exclusive labels. For instance, the physical challenges of reservists will often be linked to emotional problems, and the emotional challenges of reservists' families will often be linked to relational challenges. The categories I have chosen are provided as guideposts of the circumstances rather than exact groupings.

The Iraq War has created difficult conditions for reservists and their immediate family members, because of actual or possible combat deployment stressors. Another aspect of the relatively unique challenges of the Iraq War is that it consisted of fairly new elements of warfare: urban terrain, religious personalities as major stakeholders, and fighting an ideological group rather than another country. Since the Iraq War was different from any previous U.S. war, the care needed for military reservists and their families should also be different from that provided in the past.

On the surface, some of the challenges U.S. military reservists experienced in the Iraq War were the same as most other deployed military personnel. The reservists were fighting in the same location as active duty troops seeking to accomplish the same mission. Wayne Chappelle, an Air Force clinical psychologist, describes the common situation for those serving in the Iraq War: "The remote nature of the setting combined with exposure to multiple operational stressors (e.g., long work hours, separation from family, crowding, substandard toiletry facilities), environmental stressors (i.e., heat, venomous insects and snakes, diseases), and combat-related stressors (e.g., improvised explosive devices, suicide bombers, mortar and rocket attacks, sniper fire) was physically and psychologically taxing for even the most resilient person."[5]

5. Chappelle, "Air Force Psychologist's Collaboration," 206–7.

Chappelle's comments highlight multiple operational stressors in the Iraq War that were particularly devastating, but there is another unique stressor: advanced technology has allowed us to create equipment that can generally run nonstop. Our modern day military engagements have become twenty-four-hour wars, mainly because of our sophisticated weaponry, complex computer systems, high powered airplanes, and the location of strategic military installations around the globe, crossing time zones.

The U.S. military is the most powerful in the history of the world; it engages not only in combat, but also in a host of Military Operations Other Than War (MOOTW) activities across the globe, such as humanitarian missions. Unfortunately, the propensity of citizens to join the U.S. military has declined since the middle of the 1980s.[6] The military is proportionately smaller, relative to the U.S. population, than it has ever been in its history, all while doing more now than it has ever done.

Our heavy reliance on computer-based technology in this war required that troops be available around the clock to interpret the continuous flow of information received. In fact, military personnel deployed in the Iraq War worked on average between twelve to sixteen hours each day, typically six days per week. Furthermore, many military personnel were deployed to the Iraq War between two and five times, or more. In the past, multiple deployments to any war were rare and especially rare for reservists. However, reservists have been deployed to the Iraq War on multiple occasions. The reserves deployed 247,181 (20.8 percent) to Iraq or Afghanistan; 157,140 (13.3 percent) and 90,041 (7.5 percent), respectively, had multiple deployments.[7]

It became clear early on in the Iraq war that the weapons used by the insurgents were not the only dangers facing our reservists. For example, many environmental dangers existed: heat, spiders, and infectious diseases. One danger was Iraq's temperature, which can reach 130 degrees most of the year. Even in this extreme heat military personnel were required to wear uniforms and heavy equipment that could easily increase the body temperature to 150 degrees. Another danger our reservists encountered was Iraq's spiders, which can be lethal, and have caused much physical and psychological trauma to our reservists. As a military reserve chaplain, I conducted one-on-one and group counseling sessions for soldiers returning home from combat; often reservists would discuss recurring nightmares

6. Segal and Segal, "America's Military Population," 9.

7. Powers, "Deployment Rates."

about getting bitten in their civilian homes by one of Iraq's lethal spiders. Another reason the Iraq War was uniquely challenging for our reservists was because of the infectious diseases native to that particular region. Our reservists were in constant danger of contracting unfamiliar diseases that are unknown to our immune system—for example, leishmaniasis.

> Leishmaniasis is a preventable disease native to Iraq and other parts of Southwest Asia. Spread by sandflies . . . the disease as found in Iraq presents itself in two forms. The skin form called cutaneous leishmaniasis (Baghdad Boil) causes mild to severe skin lesions that may take months to heal and may be permanently disfiguring, though highly effective treatment is available. The internal form called visceral leishmaniasis . . . [It] causes fever, weakness, wasting, an enlarged spleen, and a lowered blood count. If untreated, visceral leishmaniasis is generally fatal . . . Some service members at locations where sandfly numbers are high are reporting upwards of 100 bites per person . . . Because the incubation period (the time for getting a sandfly bite to the development of disease) can be many months, it is also possible that deployed personnel may redeploy without knowing they are infected.[8]

Why do I focus on the *negative* impact on military reservists and their family members? During times of war there are some military reservists and their families that are spared from the stressors discussed in this research and in fact may even experience growth personally and within their family unit. While those reservists are fortunate, they are few; the majority of military reserve communities[9] find themselves isolated in the midst of war, without the proper support needed while deployed to and/or returning from war's dire circumstances. Their isolation can result from wide-ranging problems: physical, depending on the geographical distance of their residence in relation to the nearest military base; spiritual, depending on how war affects their faith journey and whether they have meaningful spiritual support; emotional, depending on the support of their civilian community; and a host of other factors that will be further addressed in later chapters. Consequently, too many military reservists are unable to move forward in their lives and participate in progress, because they have suffered such a range of emotional, physical, psychiatric, relational, and spiritual wounds due to their service in the Iraq War. It is important for military reservists

8 "DoD Issues Medical Advisory on Leishmaniasis," 9.

9. The phrase "military reserve communities" refers in this volume to all reserve branches and their immediate family members negatively impacted by the Iraq War.

and their immediate family members to receive support for their personal well being, as well as to help ensure that the United States will continue to have a strong national military line of defense.[10]

The Iraq War has presented new challenges to the religious professionals charged to care for the reservists and their families. Civilian pastors may not be familiar with military life. Military chaplains may have lost touch with the particularities of civilian life. Furthermore, there exists only minimal partnership between the military and civilian pastors, though such partnership could vastly improve care to military reservists and their families. There are limited military services that help support military reservists and their families, such as Military One Source, U.S. Department of Veterans Affairs, and Military Home Front. However, thousands of pastors minister in rural and small-town U.S. communities whose reservists are deploying to and returning from the Iraq War; these pastors are in need of practical theological resources and techniques to help them minister to the reservists and their families, because some of the most effective advocacy groups may find it geographically impossible to reach the thousands of reservists and their families living in Small Town, USA. Many pastors and chaplains are not familiar with these various advocacy groups that assist reservists and their families. My research is in favor of pastors and military chaplains caring for mind, body, and soul; it highlights the importance of referral to these specialized resources.

Military reservists and their family members experienced traumatic events during the Iraq War. Adequate attention should be placed upon the people who were literally on the front line and the families who were and are supporting them. A care plan is needed, because the Iraq War has changed the lives of these reservists and their families forever. The effects remain. Intentional care to assist reservists and families with the transition from war back to civilian life can be a matter of life and death. In "An American Suicide: What War Did to Jeffrey Lucey," John Judis, a visiting scholar at the Carnegie Endowment for International Peace, describes the experience of a twenty-three-year-old Marine reservist who returned home from the Iraq War.[11] Unfortunately, Jeffrey Lucey committed suicide by hanging himself in the basement of his parents' home on June 22, 2004. The Lucey family

10. U.S. Department of Defense, *Guard and Reserve Family Readiness for the Twenty-First Century*, Reserve Component Common Personnel Data System: 1998 DD-RA Year End Report, 1–2.

11. Judis, "An American Suicide." This endowment has highlighted stories of reservists' challenges during the Iraq War.

blamed a Veterans Administration medical center because it had refused further treatment for the reservist and turned him away. In "Family Settles with U.S. in Marine Suicide," Jonathan Saltzman notes the following about Jeffrey Lucey's family:

> The U.S. government has agreed to pay $350,000 to settle a federal claim by a Belchertown family who blamed Northampton VA Medical Center . . . The lawyer, Assistant US Attorney Karen L. Goodwin, said the suicide had led to improvements in how Veterans Administration medical centers treat veterans. Changes included the hiring of suicide-prevention coordinators and 100 new adjustment counselors at 207 Vet Centers. "VA, both nationally and locally, has been challenged to appreciate and meet the healthcare needs of veterans returning from the conflicts in Iraq and Afghanistan," Goodwin wrote Jan. 6 to the lawyer for Lucey's parents in a letter calling the $350,000 settlement a final offer.[12]

The story of Jeffrey Lucey is a tragic example of how reservists and their families have been negatively impacted by the Iraq War. Unfortunately, this tragic incident could have happened to any soldier, but one unique aspect of this situation is that it occurred in a civilian's residence rather than a military facility. Another significant aspect of this incident is that the U.S. government actually paid a settlement, because of negligence by the Veterans' Administration hospital. Civilians are becoming increasingly aware, in an up close and personal manner, of the visible and invisible wounds from the Iraq War. Jeffrey Lucey's situation is also significant because he was a reservist deployed to the Iraq War who returned home unable to resume his life in the midst of his civilian environment. The Associated Press published a story titled "Families Blame Vet Suicides on Lack of VA Care"[13] and listed numerous young adult reservists from across the country who committed suicide after returning from the Iraq War. I firmly believe that chaplains and pastors using a soul care approach may help prevent more such tragedies.

In my role as chaplain, I am called upon to be the last person military personnel see before departing for the Middle East and the first person they see upon returning to the United States. These outbound and inbound flights are often shared by reservists and active duty personnel. There is

12. Saltzman, "Family Settles with US in Marine Suicide." The *Globe* has published several stories of reservists' challenges.

13. Associated Press, "Families Blame Vet Suicides."

not a visible distinction on their uniforms to designate reservists from active duty soldiers, so the only way one would know is through verbal communication in the form of a briefing before boarding the plane and/or one-on-one conversations. My personal feelings are a combination of pride and concern for the soldiers. I am proud of our brave men and women who deploy to Iraq. I also am concerned for their safety. My experiences before the soldiers deploy include talking with them, praying for them, shaking their hands, and counseling them. I give the soldiers words of encouragement and inspiration. My perception of the soldiers is that they are ready, willing, and able to answer the call of duty to serve their country—even when the call is as difficult as deploying to the Iraq War. In my experience, the reservists and the active duty soldiers realize there are minimal differences between their duties when they board the plane bound for the Iraq War.

I have found many important issues faced by military reservists, their families, their pastors and chaplains, and the communities in which they reside. The following two questions represent the fundamental issues in constant need of attentive responses by pastors and chaplains: How can military reservists, whether deployed or not yet deployed—and their immediate family members—stay strong or at least stable during a war? How can others, especially religious professionals and communities, support them during a war? An investigation of the full range of emotional, physical, psychiatric, relational, and spiritual problems caused by the Iraq War will help military chaplains, pastors, and other practitioners provide care to reservists and their families.

A Discussion Regarding Soul Care

Will a holistic soul care approach guide chaplains and pastors in providing effective care for reservists and their families? I will argue that because a large number of reservists and their families are in a precarious situation, suffering from a wide spectrum of wounds—physical and psychiatric, emotional and relational, and spiritual—there needs to be a dedicated and broad-spectrum form of support offered by chaplains and pastors to care for them.

Soul care—*cura animarum*—is ancient nomenclature for the art of Christian pastoral care. Thomas Moore—psychotherapist and former Roman Catholic priest—describes soul and care of the soul: "Soul is not a thing, but a quality or a dimension of experiencing life and ourselves. It has to do with depth, value, relatedness, heart, and personal substance . . . Care of the soul begins with observances of how the soul manifests itself and how it operates . . . It means to watch out for but also to keep and honor, as in the observance of a holiday . . . It has to do with modest care and not miraculous cure."[14]

Moore also addresses what happens when the soul is not being cared for: "when soul is neglected, it doesn't just go away; it appears symptomatically in obsessions, addictions, violence, and loss of meaning."[15] The suggestions for soul care throughout this project are intended to be both strategic and thoughtful; they are strategic in intentionally utilizing various ways to connect with reservists and their families; they are thoughtful in that they deliberately avoid glorifying war or demonizing the enemy. The particular approach to soul care I am recommending takes into consideration Miroslav Volf's warning: "The temptation to misuse religion to legitimize violence is greatest when religion is associated with power—either power to be defended or power to be acquired . . . the closer a religion is to power, the more likely will be its misuse to legitimize violence."[16] My research does not seek to legitimize violence, but it seeks to care for those reservists and their families who are harmed by the Iraq War's violence.

For centuries the care of souls has extended beyond faith communities gathered at synagogues, churches, or mosques. Sacred texts such as the Torah, the Bible, and the Qur'an share similar stories in which soldiers were supported by religious representatives before, during, and after combat. A few of the stories highlighted in the Bible include major historical and respected figures such as David, Moses, and Joshua related to the various battles with which they were associated. In the contemporary era, World War II drew attention to the importance of chaplains and the crucial potential of their dynamic leadership qualities.[17] It is meaningful that current military chaplains can identify the importance of their pastoral roles in the three Abrahamic religions.

A soul care approach emphasizes what has been called the "ministry of presence"—welcoming interpersonal skills, thoughtful hospitality, and attentiveness to the full range of life's values and challenges. Soul care consists

---

14. Moore, *Care of the Soul*, 5.

15. Ibid., xi.

16. Volf, "Agents of Peace," 36.

17. Oates, "Pastoral Care," 835.

of functions such as healing, sustaining, reconciling, guiding, empowering, and liberating. When practiced beyond a particular religious community, it is distinctly interreligious in nature as it is primarily concerned with the well-being of a person's soul regardless of religious affiliation or its absence. With appropriate instruction, soul care can be provided individually or corporately by religious leaders and lay members alike.

In this discussion, I am relying especially on two aspects of Howard J. Clinebell's conceptualization of soul care. First, Clinebell's focus was never on sin or illness but on the capacity of religious life and leadership to foster wholeness and growth.[18] Clinebell had great confidence in the soul's capacity and potential for growth and in the capacity and potential of religious leaders and communities to engender wholeness in the midst of brokenness. He confidently argued in support of the effectiveness of religious leaders in the midst of crisis. He recognized the special relational intimacy that can develop between suffering people and religious leaders, who have this access to people's lives because they are often within arm's reach in times of trouble and joy. "Troubled people are more apt to seek help from a clergyman than from a member of any other professional group. This puts the minister in a strategic and demanding position . . . Ministers are on the front lines in the efforts to help the burdened and the troubled."[19] Clinebell also was optimistic regarding religious communities' usefulness in helping people navigate through their life challenges: "Churches and temples collectively represent a sleeping giant, a huge potential of barely tapped resources for fostering positive mental health . . . The immense mental health contributions of organized religion will be released only as increasing numbers of churches and temples become *centers of healing and growth*—centers for healing the brokenness of individuals and relationships, and settings where persons find stimulation for lifelong growth toward their fullest humanity."[20]

Religious leaders and communities are in an excellent position to help the Iraq War's troubled reservists and their families. Faith communities have done a fairly good job of trying to bring wholeness to people who become fractured by life's headaches, heartaches, and tragedies. Clinebell

18. In addition to being drawn to his scholarly work, I am drawn to Clinebell because of commonalities in our experience: both of us have pastored United Methodist Churches, taught pastoral care and counseling classes at Claremont School of Theology, counseled clients at the Clinebell Institute, and had a formal relationship with Claremont United Methodist Church.

19. Clinebell, *Mental Health Ministry*, 211.

20. Clinebell, "Local Church's Contributions," 46–47.

did not limit the church's usefulness to a narrow conception of spiritual life. Instead, he was attuned to the multidimensional nature of the human experience. The care that religious communities provide for persons and families is often long-lasting (across generations) and well rounded, marking the common passages of life—birth, love, death. Clinebell elaborates:

> Churches have always been major contributors to personality health . . . Without the stabilizing, undergirding, nurturing, value-supporting ministries of the churches, millions of persons in every age would have been diminished in their abilities to handle life situations constructively. Further, they would have been much more vulnerable to mental, emotional, and spiritual illnesses.[21]

This brings us to a second focus that makes Clinebell's view of soul care so valuable for my work. Clinebell's focus was always on the holistic nature of well being through soul care. Addressing the care seeker directly, he explains the importance of not being one–dimensional, not exclusively focusing on the body, mind, or spirit but, instead, providing care to one's entire personhood: "As a person of infinite worth and rich possibilities for enjoying more whole-person fitness, you deserve effective self-healing, loving self-care, and an alive body-mind-spirit."[22]

Especially as his scholarship and practice matured, Clinebell emphasized the holistic nature of the soul and of soul care, recognizing that the dimensions of life are not separate but interrelated. All of our experiences and the contexts in which we have those experiences affect the state of the soul—body, mind, emotions, relationships, work, play, and world. Thus, soul care ought to be intentionally holistic, seeking to raise awareness of the need for and availability of care relative to all dimensions of the human experience, emotional, physical, psychiatric, relational, or explicitly religious or spiritual. Clinebell's work helps us see soul care as attending not only to religious concerns but to the full spectrum of the human experience, since all of it affects the state of the soul and affords a means by which chaplains and pastors can assist reservists and their families as they address the wide range of problems they face during periods of combat and war. It is not that Clinebell underemphasized the profundity of the soul's suffering. Rather, his holistic view enabled him to articulate both the anguish and the transformation that crises and grief can bring. "Crises and griefs are like that. The blades of the pain cut deep channels through our souls. The plow

21. Clinebell, *Mental Health Ministry*, 13.
22. Clinebell, *Well Being*, 303.

also cuts the roots of our comfortable beliefs and life-styles. But, by the very turbulence, it also prepares the soil to nurture new seeds."[23]

Thus, soul care is an effective approach for care of reservists and their families, because it is a multifaceted approach that addresses the multiple dimensions of a person's and family's well-being in order to acknowledge the complexities of life. As he again addresses the person in need, we can overhear Clinebell articulate for us the ultimate goal of holistic care—care that is so multidimensional that those in need feel wholly cared for in the midst of multidimensional crises: "First, caring people who can hold up a light for you by supporting and loving you in your darkness . . . The second thing needed is some sense of meaning in your crisis . . . The third thing needed is some small hope for a better future."[24] The general goal of this soul care approach is to alleviate suffering in the full range of challenges experienced by the military reservist community caused by actual and possible deployments to the Iraq War.

To be fair to Clinebell, it is worth noting that my reliance on his work is a bit ironic. Clinebell did not devote attention to military chaplaincy in his research. This was likely because of his concern about the dangers of nuclear war, which led him to be highly invested in peacemaking. As one example of this commitment, Clinebell in 1984 hosted a conference at Claremont School of Theology called "Global Peacemaking and Wholeness: Developing Justice-Based Theological, Psychological and Spiritual Resources," the objectives of which included: "to increase understanding of the profound spiritual emptiness, ethical confusion, psychic numbing, and idolatry of military power underlying the present world situation with its deadly nuclear arms race threatening the human family with genocide."[25]

Nonetheless, given Clinebell's commitment to holistic conceptualization and practice for all persons, it is fair to assert that he would support the reliance on his views by military chaplains and pastors seeking to offer full-spectrum soul care to reservists and their families.

An article in the *Dictionary of Pastoral Care and Counseling* describes military chaplaincy as a cooperative arrangement between religious faith groups and the government to provide ministry to persons in the military environment.[26] There is a study indicating that an important percentage

23. Ibid., 210.
24. Ibid., 216.
25. Clinebell, "Global Peacemaking and Wholeness Conference," 1.
26. Starling, "Military Service and Military Chaplaincy," 726.

of soldiers and their families consult military chaplains and civilian clergy for help in their time of need in relation to the Iraq War.[27] One aspect of chaplains' unique responsibility in the military environment includes caring for military families. Veterans Administration Hospitals also provide chaplaincy service, though chaplains in that setting may be civilians. Chaplain Dalene C. Fuller Rogers depicts the chaplain's exceptional role in caring for combat veterans: "I believe that through the process of speaking or "confessing" these acts [in combat] to a chaplain, who does not get up and leave or condemn or rationalize them, the veteran is given an opportunity to confront the feelings he has about his behavior that he has repressed. A combat veteran may feel powerless to make amends for his actions and may see himself as an unforgivable participant in evil activity."[28] The chaplain is justly understood by the military command and viewed by the military community in general as one who can listen in a nonjudgmental and supportive manner. Military chaplains, VA chaplains, college chaplains on a campus with student veterans, and civilian pastors are in close proximity to reservists and their families. Clinebell's recommendations, added to the expertise of chaplains and pastors, creates a powerful resource to help aid reservists and their families negatively impacted by the Iraq War.

One important opportunity for the military chaplain is to facilitate pastoral theological reflection on war. For example, because of war's violence, it usually inundates a person's mind with an assortment of images of aggression. Some people believe there is not a role for aggression in religious life. Pastoral theologian and caregiver Kathleen J. Greider holds an opposing view and argues that "aggression can be cared for through spiritual practice . . . in corporate religious life. First, the silence in religious communities about aggression can be—and needs to be—broken . . . An especially rich arena of congregational life where we can care for aggression is in collective nonviolent resistance and other forms of activism . . . Spiritual disciplines offer a multitude of ways that faithful people can lend nonviolent but direct, vigorous action on behalf of important issues in church and society."[29]

Aggression is a reality of the human experience. War is a product of aggression that, whatever one's theological view of war, continues to be a reality in the human experience. My research embraces Greider's proposal

---

27. Hoge, Castro, and Eaton, "Impact of Combat Duty," 5–4.

28. Rogers, *Pastoral Care for Post-Traumatic Stress Disorder*, 45.

29. Greider, *Reckoning with Aggression*, 116.

for faith communities to engage the reality of aggression rather than ignore and avoid it. Faith communities can create a safe place to discuss the reality of aggression along with a safe space to practice aggression in helpful ways. A few ways that aggression can be practiced and reduced are through exercise, sports, candid discussions, and/ or heated debates.

Similarly, military chaplains and other religious leaders can facilitate pastoral theological reflection on the naturalness and necessity of conflict. Given human imperfection and the injustices that are part of living in flawed societies, sometimes conflicts result in war. Greider also argues for the unavoidability of conflict: "Until such time that humans are perfect and cease to irritate and harm one another, peace—if we are to have it at all—will have to coexist with conflict."[30] Much conflict between nations has evolved into war, though this is not inevitable. Conflict is often perceived primarily as an unconstructive activity that should be avoided. However, conflict can actually be effective when used correctly. Greider highlights conflict as useful when handled respectfully.

> There is no peace without justice, and no justice without conflict. Everyday people contribute to the building of peace, not by avoiding conflict but by striving to be nonviolent in our conflicts and use them to increase justice. Cultural diversity in conflict practices reveals that there are many more ways of being in conflict than we had thought possible. Though at first it feels unnatural to stray from our usual ways of being in conflict, greater interculturality in conflict practices increases the likelihood of nonviolence and our realization of the Peaceable Realm.[31]

Conflict needs to be addressed differently today than it was in the past in order to have peace and to minimize war. Soul care can help soldiers pursue peace even in the midst of wartime. Justice does not bloom on its own; instead it must be nurtured, maintained, and defended.

Practical Theology Methods

Practical theology is a critical multidisciplinary form of research that focuses on the investigation of the human experience on an individual or corporate level.[32] It includes description, critical analysis, and theologi-

30. Greider, "Nonviolent Conflicts and Cultural Differences," 130.

31. Ibid., 156.

32. Woodward and Pattison, *Blackwell Reader in Pastoral and Practical Theology*, xiii.

cal reflection that lead to questioning, insights, strategies, and revisions regarding the practice of ministry and/or that seek some remedy to challenging circumstances. I employ a practical theological method of literature research and analysis regarding how the Iraq War has caused emotional, physical, psychiatric, relational, and spiritual problems for military reservists and their family members. In order to create the "thick description" prized in practical theology, I review a multidisciplinary collection of literature that addresses the experience of reservists and their families from the perspective not only of my own discipline of pastoral care and military chaplaincy but also from the perspective of the fields of psychology, military history and science, and nursing.[33] In practical theology, a component of theological reflection is to seek to identify the activity of God in and on human experiences. Though the unseen or unproven are important aspects of religious experiences, practical theology places more emphasis on what is actually proven, seen, understood, changed, and explained.[34]

My vocational experience offers an element of participatory action research.[35] I currently serve as an Air Force Chaplain Captain reservist and have been serving since 2001, prior to the Iraq War. I have not yet had the experience of those reservists who have been deployed to war, but my family and I are anticipating that I will deploy to a hostile location in the future. I have been one of the last persons the soldiers see before they deploy to the Iraq War and one of the first persons they see upon their return. My military status enables me to offer first-person perspectives on the professional experiences, attitudes, beliefs, and perceptions of military reservists and their families. Conversely, my military status also carries with it a few biases, including a pro-military stance; therefore, the scope of this research is not intended to persuade an audience on the validity of the military, military chaplaincy, or war. My role as a reservist is important to every aspect of my research—methods, objective, insight, and experience. Pastoral theologian Emmanuel Y. Lartey describes the importance of the researcher's location relative to the topic being investigated: "[Practical Theology] raises methodological questions and realizes that it is important to have and use

33. Browning, *Fundamental Practical Theology*, 6–9.

34. Heitink, *Practical Theology*, 178–79.

35. The Center for Collaborative Action Research at Pepperdine University has given attention to participatory action research, and the findings can be found at http://cadres. pepperdine.edu/ccar/index.html. Kurt Zadek Lewin, a German-American psychologist, is accredited as one of the founders of participatory action research, in the early 1900s. Some of Lewin's work can be explored in Smith, "Kurt Lewin."

the right tools for any job. In addition, it asks questions about *who* it is that are engaged in the theological tasks, what the social locations of the persons are, *who benefits from what is done*, who is *excluded* by the way things are done and who are oppressed by it. It asks contextual and experiential questions and challenges historical formulations in a quest for more inclusive and relevant forms."[36] My practical theological method reveals the context through the detail of demographics and the experience of military reservists and their family members during the Iraq War. This practical theological analysis, informed by study of the multifaceted problems of the military reservists and their family members, serves as a foundation for an appropriate soul care approach during war.

Review of Related Literature in Pastoral Care and Counseling

There is not a large quantity of literature on chaplains' pastoral care and counseling in the midst of combat and war, especially for military reservists and their families, who are the focus of my research. However, it is useful to survey the available literature as a base of information regarding this difficult ministry. My review covers literature regarding chaplains' historical role in war and combat situations, chaplains' first-person accounts in combat and war experiences, military and government publications, articles in general magazines/newspapers written by chaplains themselves and by reporters interviewing chaplains, and pastoral care and counseling regarding military chaplaincy.

A few chaplains who have served in the Iraq War have written memoirs and other first-person accounts regarding their experiences. However, scholarly literature by specialists in the field of pastoral care and counseling, or literature offering a practical theological analysis of care by military chaplains and pastors for Iraq War–era military reservists and their families, is nonexistent. Reasons for this shortage of literature can only be surmised. But I believe that, first of all, chaplains in the military tend to be professionals whose attention is devoted to practicing the art of chaplaincy; they tend to give little time and attention to developing theory related to their professional practice. The subject of military chaplaincy has not attracted the attention of those institutions that provide the financial support that makes research and writing possible—schools, foundations, denominations, etc.

36. Lartey, "Practical Theology as a Theological Form," 131.

We can also assume that theological reasons underlie the fact that military chaplaincy (like prison chaplaincy) gets little attention in research and publication, especially as compared to hospital chaplaincy. War and combat are complex and contentious topics in religious circles; many civilians are uncomfortable with or uncommitted to the military's harsh realities. Thus, too many faith communities do not mention these issues, much less wrestle with these particular realities in our society. Ironically, the Bible is replete with accounts of war, many of which were stated to have divine sanction.

Some literature addresses the work of chaplains in recent years; other texts address a chaplain's care of war veterans and their families after returning from deployment. I have reviewed those texts that give voice directly to chaplains, those with experience working with chaplains, and those who have interviewed chaplains. I analyze the literature from the perspective of my experience as an Air Force chaplain reservist and a United Methodist pastor. A prayer from my faith tradition is titled "For Those in Military Service" and includes these words: "Righteous God, you rule the nations. Guard brave men and women in military service. Give them compassion for those who confront them as enemies . . . Though for a season they must be people of war, let them live for peace, as eager for agreement as for victory . . ."[37]

Pastoral care and counseling is displayed in various ways and serves multiple purposes in the reserves. Chaplain Rodney Miller, former Division Support Command Chaplain of the 28th Infantry Division, Pennsylvania National Guard, writes: "The chaplain in a reserve component unit can have a major impact upon the stress level in his or her unit through the following pastoral care offered: 1. The personal identity of the chaplain; 2. The worship service and preaching; 3. The teaching offered by the chaplain; 4. The advising of the commander and staff by the chaplain; 5. The chaplain's presence and visitation; 6. The chaplain's personal and family counseling and pastoral conversation."[38] In Miller's list, the potential impact of a chaplain's pastoral care and counseling looks very similar to the potential impact of a civilian pastor.[39] Nonetheless, though the acts may be similar, the context in which they are carried out is extremely different. Miller focuses upon the reservists' challenges in balancing civilian commitments

---

37. United Methodist Church, *United Methodist Book of Worship*, 541.

38. Miller, "In Two Worlds," 13.

39. The fourth item is an obvious exception—"The advising of the commander and staff . . ."

along with military commitments. He highlights dynamics that reservists and their families experience during peacetime and war. Unfortunately, however, Miller does not discuss in great detail how the context of war and combat affect the work of the chaplain.

Naomi Paget, a professor at Golden Gate Theological Seminary and Denver Seminary, and Janet McCormack, a retired Air Force chaplain, have written a book titled *The Work of the Chaplain*. The book highlights different chaplaincy professions—military chaplaincy, health care chaplaincy, and prison chaplaincy, among others—while briefly yet respectfully exploring their broad responsibilities. They acknowledge how the chaplain as caregiver is also in need of self-care;[40] however, their scope is broad, whereas my research exclusively focuses upon military chaplains and pastors, offering an in-depth investigation into reservists and their families in relation to the Iraq War.

One book that I have found particularly useful is *Under Orders: A Spiritual Handbook for Military Personnel* by William McCoy, an active duty Army chaplain. McCoy gives a multidimensional look at combat's influence in various aspects of the soldier's life, though is main purpose seems to be to assist a young generation of soldiers with finding their true selves in a morally based philosophy and theology with a preference toward Christianity. One finds throughout McCoy's text a variety of philosophies of life, various cultures, religions, and traditions, as well as numerous references to popular movies, books, and media outlets, which he incorporates intentionally in order to reach younger generations.[41]

The primary focus of my research is on reservists and their families. Although it is clear that they are not primary in McCoy's agenda, he gives a brief overview in a few paragraphs about the reserve community: "For the first time since Vietnam and the Gulf War, the Coast Guard is deploying to the Near East. Everyone is involved including National Guard soldiers at home and serving in rotations abroad . . . Military service today comes with the certain promise of deploying to hostile fire zones. And there is no sign that this will change in the near term."[42] McCoy does not go into extensive detail about the negative impact on individual reservists and/or their families, which is another emphasis of my research. "As we go along in the war on terror and in Iraq in particular, we are realizing that our people

40. Paget and McCormack, *Work of the Chaplain*, 114.
41. McCoy, *Under Orders*, 37.
42. Ibid., 155.

still get shot, maimed, blown up and killed in spite of all advantages. And that realization makes these days all the more difficult mentally, emotionally and spiritually."[43] He describes scores of other challenges such as sexism, racism, adultery, murder, identity crises, sin, and death that civilian young people experience and soldiers encounter, but he does not provide any comprehensive plans or a systematic approach of assisting reservists and/or their families to address their issues.

McCoy gives personal accounts of how the media in relation to the Iraq War has negatively affected his family and how the media can negatively impact other military communities. Still, he does not recommend many alternatives for military families with deployed members to manage media coverage of combat.

> . . . CNN came on the radio with a report from Fallujah where my son was a Platoon Leader with the Marine infantry . . . [my wife] recognized the voice of [our] son. In that moment, she collapsed her head on her desk in tears realizing the closeness of combat had reached even to her desk . . . This is the weirdness of combat in this digital age . . . The fact is combat stress extends over our families at home in a greater way than we ever realized. Every spouse, child, parent and sibling of the deployed force is in combat vicariously.[44]

McCoy offers a list of good questions at the end of each chapter that are philosophical, religious, spiritual and theological in nature. He intends for the reader to seriously consider God's presence and God's activity in the world and one's own stance regarding those sacred dynamics. An aspect of McCoy's book that is similar to my research is his attention to the significance of the soul—especially the soldiers' soul during war. McCoy identifies the military community as plagued by loneliness that causes emotional stress and negatively impacts the soul. He recognizes that souls can become wounded in many ways during war.

In *Ministry with the Military: A Guide for Churches and Chaplains*, Donald W. Hadley and Gerald T. Richards recommend that churches offer support to the military community. They also propose that churches partner with civilian organizations to provide other forms of specialized care.[45] They primarily focus on how churches that are geographically located near active duty bases can help minister to soldiers. However, they do not men-

43. Ibid., 221.
44. Ibid., 236.
45. Hadley and Richards, *Ministry with the Military*, 50.

tion reservists and their families—the special challenges they face—nor do they offer suggestions as to how to care for them.

In *Counseling the Serviceman and His Family,* Thomas A. Harris writes a book that is a product of its time—1964—in that it exclusively focuses upon the male as the military spouse and does not make any mention of the complexities of single parenting,[46] in securing a safe residence for children while one or both parents deploy. The primary purpose of Harris' book is for a time of peace, in contrast to my research, which principally focuses upon the military community during a time of war. Furthermore, his text does not include the reserves and/or their families in the discussion.

Deann Alford's article titled "Faith, Fear, War, Peace: Snapshots of the Grim and 'Happy' Ministry of Today's Military Chaplains" is similar to my research in that it highlights challenges that chaplains encounter in the Iraq War, including proximity to combat. Chaplains' official non-combatant status does not guarantee they will not get injured while serving. Another similarity of Alford's article in relation to my research is that she also highlights some of the perils of reservists in the Iraq War. For example, she includes experiences of Sergeant Livier Lazaro, who directed an aid station and trauma center in the Iraq War: "Few soldiers killed in Iraq have open-casket funerals. We saw people blown up. We carried body parts . . . The hardest part was losing civil affairs reservist Nicole Frye, 19, of Lena, Wisconsin. Frye died February 16 [2004] when a roadside bomb hit her Humvee just 10 days after she arrived in Iraq. Lazaro helped remove her remains from the vehicle. Lazaro had never before encountered a mortally wounded female soldier."[47]

However, Alford's article does not explore the multidimensional suffering of reservists or their families in relation to the Iraq War, such as their emotional, psychiatric, and/or spiritual problems.

In Frank Brown's article titled "Ministering to an Unpopular War," he gives attention to some reserve chaplains who graduated from Yale Divinity School, and he includes some rare dissention by chaplains in relation to the Iraq War. Brown sheds light on one chaplain's candid theological struggle with some of the military's operations. He reveals Army National Guard chaplain Lee Hardgrove's feelings about his involvement with the Iraq War: "At the age of 54 and with misgivings about the course of the United States-led global war on terror . . . I prayed—but not out of being a coward—not

---

46. Harris, *Counseling the Serviceman and His Family.*

47. Alford, "Faith, Fear, War, Peace," 47.

to go to Iraq. I didn't feel comfortable. I felt I was over my head in the task I was being given. And from the just war theological side, I wasn't comfortable . . . The Lord blessed me and sent me to Afghanistan."[48] Brown does not describe the way(s) in which the reserve chaplains' deployment(s) have impacted their civilian churches. This is an interesting topic for me, because I am currently serving simultaneously as Senior Pastor of a United Methodist Church and as an Air Force reservist chaplain. I believe I am a better civilian pastor because of my military chaplaincy and vice versa. Though it is beyond the scope of this project, that particular issue is worth exploring, especially as to how reservists representing other professions (besides chaplaincy) and/or their families have been impacted by the Iraq War.

Wayne Chappelle's article titled "An Air Force Psychologist's Collaboration with Clergy: Lessons Learned on the Battlefield of Iraq" does not give attention to the reserves and/or their families. Nonetheless, Chappelle's article is similar to my research regarding the value of utilizing an interdisciplinary approach to care for soldiers in the Iraq War. He acknowledges that many soldiers encounter multiple challenges in mental health, physical health, and spiritual health.[49] He understands that war's traumatic effects on soldiers should not and/or cannot be resolved exclusively by one professional. Chappelle's article acknowledges the chaplains' significance during the Iraq War:

> One of the most relied upon and trusted helping agents on the battlefield are members of the clergy. Their duties include, but are not limited to: individual and unit worksite visitations, attendance at organizational functions (e.g., giving an opening prayer for an event), guidance on religious and spiritual issues, counseling to provide emotional support for those struggling with grief and loss over the death of a comrade, brief forms of crisis intervention, participating in death notifications, and performing a general "ministry of presence." . . . Historically, members of the clergy have served as healers of emotional distress well before psychologists; and in many cases continue to occupy such a position among many military personnel.[50]

---

48. Brown, "Ministering to an Unpopular War," 4.

49. Chappelle, "Air Force Psychologist's Collaboration," 209–10.

50. Ibid., 208.

Among Chappelle's primary points are that chaplains are of major importance during war; other professionals can learn from chaplains, just as chaplains learn from other professions; and all professions should partner with one another in order to enhance care for soldiers during war.

John DeVelder's article titled "The Effects of War on Pastoral Care and Counseling" focuses upon a reservist in the National Guard, Chaplain Lieutenant Colonel Joanne Martindale, and her deployments to the Iraq War. The article briefly mentions some of the difficulties Chaplain Martindale encountered by leaving her husband and two children during her deployment to the Iraq War. However, the article places the greatest importance on Chaplain Martindale's recommendation for veterans to receive better care when they return from war: "much needs to be done to help returning veterans as they reenter civilian life . . . the two most important words for a vet to hear upon return are 'Welcome home' . . . 'Welcome home' is not always the experience of some troops . . . some soldiers who need treatment for PTSD (post-traumatic stress disorder) and do not receive the psychological help they need. She mentioned that congregations can help but that finding the vet to offer support and care is not often easy . . ."[51] DeVelder does not go into any detail or in-depth discussion of possible solutions as to how congregations or other communities can offer support to veterans returning to civilian life, but he does a good job of disclosing how an actual reservist chaplain engages in the complexities of the Iraq War.

Cecile S. Landrum's article "The Changing Military Family: An Increased Role for the Chaplain" highlights the chaplain's role as pivotal in the military community. Landrum's text emphasizes how military families are becoming increasingly dysfunctional, but are often resistant in seeking help for fear of being subjected to stigmatization within the military. Therefore, chaplains' ministry of care to military personnel and/or their families often extends beyond the spiritual realm of difficulties and into other non-spiritual areas of concern. Landrum explains: "As chaplains know, many families are not coping, and one result of this inability to deal with the stress is apparent in the growing incidence of family violence in the military. It is apparent that too many families are either afraid of the connotations of seeking mental health care or are just plain unwilling to seek help until family problems become crises."[52] Landrum understands that chaplains are among the few professional officers who are on the front

---

51. DeVelder, "Effects of War on Pastoral Care and Counseling."
52. Landrum, "Changing Military Family," 5.

lines with soldiers. They usually have more time and a closer relationship with the majority of soldiers than other combat support professional officers, such as psychologists, psychiatrists, other mental health practitioners, and physicians. One contributing factor is that chaplains usually take the initiative to visit the soldiers, while the other professional officers generally wait for the soldiers to visit them.

As an Air Force chaplain reservist, I make as many pastoral visits to as many soldiers as I can on the military base. My mental health colleagues' work rhythm and expectations are different from my chaplaincy profession. For instance, soldiers are required to see the medical physician a few times a year for various checkups. They also receive annual training sessions from a mental health professional about a particular subject, such as suicide prevention or drug abuse. However, it is not customary for mental health practitioners and doctors to be as mobile, present, and engaged with the soldiers as the chaplain. Another factor is that most soldiers are more comfortable and familiar with chaplains than with other combat support professional officers. Also, soldiers' interaction with the chaplain is confidential and not recorded, as is required with a physician, psychologist and/ or psychiatrist.

In Isaac Olivarez's "Pastoring the Air Force's 'Pastors,'" he highlights the fact that military chaplains have an obligation to provide pastoral care and counseling in the midst of conflicts and war. If the world insists on war, it is in desperate need of, and has a place for, a pastoral presence in the midst of that chaos. Soldiers, including chaplains, do not have the luxury to decide whether or not they will enter war, as they have sworn an oath to military service which is not predicated upon their personal preferences. War is glorious or glamorous only to people who are not familiar with battle and its scars.

In Robert Phillips' "The Military Chaplain in Time of War: Contours and Content of Ministry," he focuses upon the responsibilities of chaplains' pastoral care and counseling, which includes counseling soldiers' families on the home front, assisting these families to find the appropriate resources for their particular needs, and constantly advising commanders on religious, spiritual, and moral issues. Phillips' text informs the reader that chaplains' care for soldiers in the midst of combat is an important aspect, but it is only one essential aspect of their pastoral role within the military. Philips explains: "Ministry in combat is not a static snapshot but a holistic, seamless approach that begins well before hostilities commence. It includes gatherings with families of those about to depart for the combat zone . . . Chaplains, whether deployed or remaining at the home bases, are key players in this human preparation for the uncertainty of what awaits."[53] Chaplains' pastoral care and counseling are usually needed by military reservists and their families during the three major phases of military operations: pre-deployment, deployment, and post-deployment.

Chaplain James A. Edgren's article "Military Chaplains" describes how the performance of pastoral care and counseling within military situations is closely related to chaplains' physical fitness. Chaplains must be physically fit in order to remain in a position to offer pastoral care and counseling. Personally, I have supervisors who continually remind me of the necessity for chaplains to stay physically fit. Indeed, in 2010, the Air Force Reserve increased physical fitness tests from once a year to twice a year to help ensure that all military personnel remain battle ready at all times. Thus, I take a physical fitness test twice a year that consists of doing push-ups and sit-ups, as well as running a mile and a half. I take this physical fitness test along with other soldiers regardless of religious affiliation, rank, or professional expertise. Chaplains are evaluated in terms of their job performance, but their required physical fitness is one major factor that distinguishes them from other pastoral professions, such as hospital chaplains, college chaplains, and civilian pastors. The significant difference is that a chaplain must be physically fit for combat and war in order to remain a military chaplain. Edgren explains: "Combat tests the limits of human endurance and quickly brings soldiers, sailors, airmen, and marines back to the basic, essential questions of life. In a life-threatening environment of maximum stress, opportunities for life-changing ministry are limited only by the chaplain's physical endurance and spiritual stamina. It is for this reason that chaplains undergo the same rigorous training and must maintain the level of physical fitness as the service members to whom they minister."[54]

In Ira C. Starling Jr.'s text "Military Service and Military Chaplaincy," he compares and contrasts some aspects of a military chaplain's ministry and a civilian ministry: "The sacramental, liturgical, and pastoral work of military chaplains is identical to that of civilian clergy. Where the military ministry is different, it reflects the following unique features of the military environment: mobility, young adults, field operations, religious pluralism,

---

53. Phillips, "Military Chaplain in Time of War," 51.
54. Edgren, "Military Chaplains," 449–50.

and institutional concerns."[55] While chaplains are required to be endorsed by their faith community, they are responsible to care for all soldiers, which is another distinction between a chaplain's care in the military and a pastor's responsibility in a local church. For example, a pastor can refuse care to a lay person or remove a lay person from church membership. Military chaplains often care for soldiers and their families who are not of the same religious faith tradition. They do not attempt to persuade military personnel to transition from one faith tradition to another faith tradition. Theological disputes and/or doctrinal differences become secondary and/or irrelevant to military chaplains. What becomes primary is the complexity of military life and the various wounds caused by military conflict that negatively impacts people of all theological and doctrinal traditions.

55. Starling, "Military Service and Military Chaplaincy," 727.

Chapter 2

The Chaplain in Wartime and Combat

CHAPLAINS ARE NOT EXCLUDED from combat and war. In fact, the pastoral care and counseling provided by chaplains become even more critical, in order for most soldiers to experience comfort and meaning during these difficult times. This chapter explores the pastoral presence of chaplains during times of war; their influence on soldiers and their family members and military leaders, as well as ways chaplains are influenced by war. I will examine chaplains' participation in various wars such as the Civil War, Spanish-American War, World War I, World War II, Korean War, Vietnam War, and Iraq War. This assessment will further advance my argument of the significance of chaplains' care within the military.

There are vast distinctions between ordinary military life and participation in warfare. Robert Gushwa describes how chaplains' duties during combat and war differ from their duties during peacetime: "The principal differences between chaplain activities in combat and those during training periods were that in combat, a) chaplains operated on an irregular schedule; b) the men were continually conscious of the possibility of death and were inclined to give more serious attention to religion; c) the wounded became an important part of the chaplain's concern; d) caring for the dead and assisting in graves registration was an added responsibility; e) religious ministrations were conducted with a minimum of shelter and equipment."[1] Since chaplains' activities in combat and war differ considerably from those

1. Gushwa, *Best and Worst of Times,* 147.

in peacetime, it may be that a person can be an effective peacetime chaplain and not be an effective combat chaplain.

During wartime, chaplains work around the clock to make themselves available for all soldiers, whether they are preparing to deploy, have deployed, or are returning from deployment. Depending on where the chaplain is serving, the chaplain's work generally includes conducting worship services, religious devotions, pastoral visitations, eulogies, and advising commanders.

War or war-related activities are of course unavoidable for soldiers. Chaplain Major General Cecil Richardson, Chief of Chaplains for the U.S. Air Force, shared his vision in 2004: "Two primary things distinguish us from civilian ministry. We're deployable—that is, we can be sent anywhere in the world at a moment's notice—and we're trained to survive in a combat environment. I constantly look at training to make sure Air Force chaplains are not a liability to the commanders but an asset. One of my top priorities is to get chaplains into areas where soldiers are in harm's way so they have access to a chaplain. I want to ensure our young men and women have somebody who will pray for them and be their pastor as they serve their country in dangerous and hostile places."[2] As Chaplain Richardson notes, whether active duty or reserve, military chaplains must be prepared to deploy suddenly, anywhere in the world. His insight about chaplains being an asset and not a liability is significant, because a chaplain's care for soldiers must not be contradictory to the military's mission under the particular commander. Therefore, the pastoral care and counseling provided by the chaplain are greatly influenced by the military's specific wartime mission.

Duties and Expectations of the Chaplain in Wartime and Combat

Nulvin S. Sauds' book titled *Chaplains' Spiritual Ministry for All Faiths in War Emergency* focuses upon the inspirational role of pastoral care and counseling to soldiers during war. Pastoral care and counseling includes a variety of methods by which the caregiver tries to comfort, challenge, confront, educate, and instruct. Pastoral care and counseling also has other methods for specific settings. For example, when engaged in battle, chaplains are expected to assist in accomplishing the objective of the U.S. military to win the war. Sauds suggests how a chaplain's pastoral care and counseling can be guided in the midst of war: "All religious ministrations

2. Olivarez, "Pastoring the Air Force's 'Pastors.'"

must be made with one thought in mind, namely to bring encouragement, cheer and confidence and to remove all fear, leaving the man courageous and unafraid . . . Even in the most serious cases, cheer and confidence must be the governing factors."[3] This is a tall order for chaplains to fulfill during war situations—it may be difficult to achieve. The task is not easy, but chaplains are expected to provide care and inspiration in valleys of the shadow of death during war—without any or minimal fear. World War II offers a story about four chaplains onboard a sinking ship, the USS Dorchester: two Protestant pastors, a Catholic priest, and a Jewish rabbi were among the first on deck, calming the men and handing out life jackets. When the jackets ran out, they took off their own and placed them on waiting soldiers without regard to faith or race. All four chaplains died together while holding one another's hands in the sinking of their ship, because they elected to put the soldiers' safety first.[4] Bravery and courage win wars, so commanders expect chaplains to help project those expressions with the intent that other soldiers will follow along those lines.

Chaplains are not exclusively pro-combat or pro-war, but neither can they be exclusively anti-combat or anti-war and expect to remain in service as a military chaplain. Therefore, the pastoral care and counseling that chaplains provide in the midst of combat and war is adaptable to the environment. Navy chaplain Louis V. Iasiello wrote: "As chaplains, our responsibility is to help our people understand the moral basis for engaging in war, the moral limitations on the methods of war, and the moral dangers involved for participants in war."[5] If chaplains do not accept combat and war as a necessary reality, they are neglecting one of the military's primary objectives. They most likely will be viewed as irrelevant or ineffective, and they may be removed from military service. A critical mission of chaplains' pastoral duties includes embodying conduct that will encourage soldiers. As Roy Honeywell noted, "Every attempt to evaluate the chaplain's work must consider the effect of military life and participation in warfare upon the soldier."[6]

---

3. *Chaplains' Spiritual Ministry for All Faiths in War Emergency*, 1. This booklet was apparently issued to U.S. military chaplains during World War II. A rabbi who served as a chaplain during that war gave his copy to Claremont School of Theology Library.

4. Immortal Chaplains Foundation, "Story of the Four Immortal Chaplains."

5. Iasiello, "Chaplain as Noncombatant," 50.

6. Honeywell, *Chaplains of the United States Army*, 340.

Combat and war conditions heighten the intensity and the necessity of the chaplain's pastoral care and counseling. The chaplain's approach to soldiers during war typically varies according to the chaplain's ministry style, faith tradition, and combat situation. There may be moments in war when soldiers and their families can enjoy meaningful reflection about the world in which they live that brings them significant peace. Chaplains may also find time to take pleasure in their ministry, as they preach and baptize members of the military community. However, chaplains and others in the military community experience many somber moments. For example, allow us to consider the unique pastoral style of Chaplain William Corby, who was a Roman Catholic chaplain during the Civil War:

> Late in the afternoon of July 2, 1863, the Irish Brigade was ordered to advance and meet the attacking Confederate force. Before the soldiers went forward, however, Corby climbed onto a nearby boulder and, exposing himself to enemy fire, stood up and pronounced the absolution of sin on every man he saw. He later claimed that all the soldiers in the brigade, whether Catholic or not, knelt solemnly in front of him as cannonballs exploded and bullets whistled over their heads. Sustained by their own prayers and by the priest's benediction, the troops then joined the battle and bravely risked death in defense of the Union position. The Irish Brigade and the other units supporting it blunted the Confederate assault against Cemetery Ridge and Little Round Top, and Gettysburg ultimately became the most significant Union victory in the war. Veterans of the Irish Brigade never forgot the courage their chaplain had displayed . . . they erected a bronze statue of the priest . . . on the Gettysburg battlefield.[7]

Many chaplains will not seek to influence the resolve of soldiers in such an extraordinary manner as Chaplain Corby. Indeed, questions can be appropriately raised about the honor given to Corby: for example, would he have a statue in his honor if his Irish Brigade had not been victorious? Questions such as this underline the importance of the clearly defined role and appropriate expectations of the chaplain. The effectiveness of a chaplain's pastoral style should not be measured by soldiers' successes or defeats.

7. Shattuck, "Faith, Morale, and the Army Chaplain," 112–13.

Ministry of Presence

Many soldiers desire to have a chaplain physically present during combat and war. The chaplain's presence helps soldiers maintain a feeling of the rightness of their mission. In fact, the mere presence of a chaplain can provide a sense of approval and assuredness to the soldiers concerning the acts they will carry out—whether it is military police providing security in hostile environments, pilots initiating air strikes, infantrymen shooting, and/or physicians performing complex surgical procedures. This desire is similar to some parishioners' desire to have a clergyperson present at the hospital during surgery, when a baby is born, in a courtroom during a trial, or in other challenging situations. I have been asked to fill this physical, spiritual, and symbolic role many times in my civilian ministry. In all cases, the parishioners did not expect me to provide medical assistance in the hospital or legal advice in the courtroom; instead, they sought the ministry of presence.

Nevertheless, the ministry of presence in military chaplaincy is more up close and personal than in congregational life, because chaplains share all aspects of life with the soldiers in combat zones. Chaplains eat the same meals and live in the same environment with their soldiers. Anne C. Loveland highlights the relationships formed between soldiers and chaplains:

"The 'ministry of presence' they [chaplains] provided to soldiers in the combat zone constituted their most important contribution to morale. Accompanying the men on combat missions, living in the dust and mud with them, eating the same rations, sharing the trauma and losses of battle—that of intimate association, apart from the performance of the usual priestly and pastoral duties—earned chaplains the gratitude of many enlisted men and officers."[8] Soldiers appreciate the chaplain's ministry of presence because it gives them a sense of unity with the chaplain, who symbolizes a spiritual power. In my civilian ministry, I did not eat the hospital food with my hospitalized parishioners, nor was I in the same legal troubles of my parishioners. How much more, then, can the sense of assuredness that my presence provides be magnified for the soldiers I serve.

---

8. Loveland, "From Morale Builders to Moral Advocates," 236.

Pastoral Care for the Dead and Dying

Spiritual power is arguably at its zenith when the chaplain provides pastoral care for dying and dead military personnel. Chaplains provide pastoral care for deceased soldiers by administering spiritual rites, such as reading or reciting Scripture, prayer, anointing, and other rituals. Chaplain Terence P. Finnegan's experience in World War II is recorded as follows:

"The chaplain said the last rites for the dead, drove to the hospital in an ambulance full of wounded men, and ministered there to the living and dying. Hundreds of litters—more than 400—filled the hospital. In the afternoon he went out to a plane that had crashed and burned to pull out the broken body of the pilot. He administered the last rites."[9] The prospect of death is a harsh reality in combat. Ministry with the dying and deceased is a powerful assurance to soldiers still living. Many soldiers take solace in seeing chaplains provide pastoral care to their dead and dying comrades, confidently knowing the chaplains will also provide similar pastoral care to them in the event of their own death. Military chaplains and congregational pastors are under similar expectations for pastoral care of the wounded and dead, among the chaplain's most challenging duties. However, civilian pastors do not work with constant reminders of injuries and death as do chaplains, who face the same dangers as the people for whom they provide care—bombs and snipers, among a host of other deadly threats. C. M. Drury gives one account of a chaplain's pastoral care and counseling goals achieved: "This account may be taken as typical of the activities of all Navy chaplains who lived up to the ideals and traditions of the Chaplain Corps while serving in Korea under combat conditions. [Chaplain] Austin wrote: . . . 'Since joining this battalion, I can sincerely say that none of our wounded has left the front without being seen by a chaplain . . . In four out of the eight deaths, I was able to hold a closing prayer before the men died (two Catholic and two Protestant prayers).'"[10]

A less often considered demand placed on chaplains is that in combat they frequently have to assess and provide pastoral care swiftly rather than in a contemplative or gradual manner. Practice takes precedence over theory for chaplains in the midst of combat and war. The military chaplaincy is an action-oriented ministry. It is important for chaplains to stay emotionally, physically, psychologically, relationally, and spiritually fit; if not, they

9. Jorgensen, *Service of Chaplains*, 84.

10. Drury, *History of the Chaplain Corps*, 59.

run the risk of placing themselves and their soldiers in danger, or of being sent home to the United States immediately because of their inability to handle the tempo. It is difficult to plan for rest during a combat and war schedule. A chaplain reflects on his experience in the Vietnam War: "[My] worst memories were immediate. [I] arrived in Da Nang and went straight to a Chu Lai field medical hospital, B-Med. Operation Harvest Moon was taking place. Just in the space of an hour or so, they brought in nine dead Marines, a dozen or more wounded Marines and some wounded and deceased Vietnamese people. It was chaos in the tent. This was my baptism in Vietnam."[11]

Not only do chaplains usually have to provide pastoral care in a swift manner, but they often have a very short time to develop a caring relationship with a soldier. The chaplain will often not have the luxury to schedule follow-up meetings or set long term goals with soldiers, due to the nature and uncertainty of war.

Female Chaplains

Women have always supported the U.S. military in a variety of meaningful ways, and now they are serving the military as chaplains in an exemplary manner. Female chaplains uniquely serve in two very male-dominated professions simultaneously: the military and the ministry. When raising the issue of gender in the military, female chaplains often work in the midst of sexism and systems of patriarchy. In spite of this, female chaplains rise above the inequitable and demanding circumstances to serve their country. The experience of Lieutenant Colonel Joanne Martindale, the female chaplain mentioned above, who served two tours in the Iraq War, gives us a glimpse of the significant ministry chaplains can provide in combat. " . . . a soldier called to her to ask for help. He was holding up one of his arms that had been severed in an explosion from an IED (improvised explosive device) that had blown up his Humvee. Joanne took his severed arm and held it while they waited for the surgeons to be ready to operate on the man."[12] This chaplain not only cared for soldiers who were injured, but she was also placed in dangerous scenarios where she could have been injured by soldiers as well, as the following story shows. "Many days Joanne counseled soldiers (sometimes ten hours straight) who needed to talk about their ex-

11. "Chaplains Muse on War Years."

12. DeVelder, "Effects of War on Pastoral Care and Counseling."

periences. One memorable counseling session for Joanne was with a soldier who threatened to kill his commanding officers and himself because he just couldn't take it anymore. Joanne gave the soldier care and won his confidence enough to take away his loaded gun and walk him over to the camp psychiatrist. The psychiatrist later told Joanne that she had saved three lives that day and possibly her own."[13] Chaplain Martindale was in immediate danger from a fellow soldier who could have easily killed her, but she still cared for him and fulfilled her demanding military pastoral duties.

Religious Diversity

The military is becoming increasingly sensitive to religious diversity within its ranks. A soldier's specific faith tradition, or lack of religious identity, is not a primary concern when a chaplain is providing pastoral care and counseling to soldiers, especially during combat and war. Chaplains build relationships with and provide counsel to agnostics, people of faith, and soldiers who have no specific religious identity. Chaplains' primary concern is not for a soldier's faith tradition or lack of one, but for each soldier as a person. Chaplain Carey H. Cash relates an experience that illustrates the depths of the chaplain's personal concern for each soldier: "Just then Captain Dickens updated me about the two Alpha Company casualties. There was no way I, or anyone standing with us, could have been prepared for his words. 'KIA. One of them was killed in action.' My heart sank. My impulse was to grab Dickens and shout, 'No! It's not true. Nobody's dead!' Instead I quietly asked, 'Dear God, who was it?' 'It was Shane.'"[14] Chaplains' first-person accounts of their experience in combat help us grasp this context of care. It is significant the chaplain did not verbalize his fears to the soldiers. Chaplain Cash writes of his experience in the Iraq War: "'Incoming! That was incoming!' My stomach sank and sweat began to bead up all over me, making me feel like I was being prodded and poked with tiny needles. I fumbled to get out of my sack and into my chemical protective suit—boots, mask, and gloves. I could hear myself breathing rapidly, and out of the corner of my eye I could see others doing the same things I was doing, frantically donning their chem-gear, jumping into the bottoms of their fighting holes, praying. The Iraqis were firing on us."[15] This

13. Ibid.
14. Cash, *Table in the Presence*, 78–79.
15. Ibid., 113.

example underscores the seriousness of providing pastoral care and how quickly life circumstances can change while ministering to soldiers who are ill, diseased, injured, fatigued, and dying or dead. As an Air Force chaplain reservist, I have practiced putting on chemical gear on several occasions in preparation for my turn in war. Chaplain Cash is candid about some of his concerns during the Iraq War: "In the back of our minds I know we were all thinking the same thing: Where's the next one going to land? Many fears race through a warrior's heart and mind on the field of battle. What if I get shot? What if I'm ambushed? Will I see terrible suffering? Will I get separated from my unit? Will I live or die? . . . But without a doubt, the greatest psychological turmoil and intense fear was caused by incoming artillery shells or rockets. The reason was simple—we couldn't see who was firing at us."[16] It is important to note that none of the previous questions were explicitly religious, not even those of the chaplain. Chaplains providing pastoral care and counseling in combat must reflect upon many issues that are not necessarily religious, spiritual, or theological. At the same time, religious practices are important to some soldiers. Chaplain Cash recounts a prayer he offered as a soldier prepared for battle: "We asked God to help him trust and believe that nothing in this world—no power, no threat, no false prediction—could ever frustrate God's perfect will from being accomplished in his life. With that, I laid my hands upon his shoulder and said, 'Go now, and do your job. Just know that God will be with you, not only during the rest of the war, but for the rest of your life.'"[17] The chaplains provide words of reassurance to soldiers to encourage them to continue their efforts and not give up. This is not a time for chaplains to give voice to fears or doubts to soldiers.

The chaplain's choice to lay his hand on the shoulder of the soldier draws our attention to the possibilities associated with a particular action often used by chaplains during combat and war: the power of touch. Touch as a part of healing has a long and important history in the Christian tradition.[18] The power of touch in the context of combat and war may seem surprising for some people. Combat tends to elicit images of bullets, bombs, heavy uniforms, weighty equipment, and other rough descriptions. Yet, these are human beings aspiring for existence and looking for meaning

16. Ibid., 114.

17. Ibid., 124.

18. Biblical texts that mention the power of touch and healing within a religious context include: 1 Kgs 17:17–23; 2 Kgs 4:32–36; Mark 8:22; and Luke 6:19.

in their combatant behavior underneath and in between the rough reality of combat and war. A chaplain wrote the following about his experience in the Iraq War: "When our time for prayer was over and it was time for the AAV to pull out, I tried, as best I could, to lay my hands on each one of them, on an arm, a shoulder, or a hand. Human touch, I found, became an all-important symbol to them, nearly sacramental in its import . . . They were desperate. And desperate men do not hunger for trivialities. They hunger for someone to point them to the One who is the Way, the Truth, and the Life. They long for a relationship with God."[19] It has often been the case, when I stood as one of the last officers in line at the military aircraft departing for Iraq, that my own life has been impacted powerfully by touch. I have found in my own ministry that the power of touch is significant to those soldiers that I hugged and shook hands with immediately prior to their boarding the plane for Iraq. The extended handshakes and hugs we exchanged were powerful and provided the soldiers one last reassurance through my presence that they were doing the "right thing" by answering the call to fight for their country and would prayerfully return safely home. Touch can transmit messages of care such as faith, hope, and support.

Chaplains are often welcomed by soldiers to speak words that can comfort under extraordinarily stressful situations. Not only can pastoral care and counseling consist of components of listening and touch, but it can also have a component of speaking. During combat and war, most sounds that are heard are strict orders, bomb or missile blasts, and screams of pain or cries of fear. Chaplains' words can offer a type of support that helps to care for the soldiers' soul. Chaplain Lance Kittleson describes the importance of caring through speech: "We need words that remind of promises given long ago; promises of the presence, promises that however our journey progresses, the living Savior will bring us safely home to his eternal presence. 'Pray, Chaplain, pray.' 'Remind us, Pastor, remind us.' 'Do not be afraid—I am with you' in the Iraqi dawn, in the fires and cauldron of all life's hazardous journeys until by the power and love of God in Christ we are safely and forever home."[20] Words spoken by chaplains should not be underestimated during combat and war. Just as the football coach or politician can energize others to act and believe in their own power, so can a chaplain serving in war time. Chaplains provide care to soldiers with words that help give encouragement and soulful nourishment. It is also

19. Cash, *Table in the Presence*, 121.

20. Kittleson, *Meditations from Iraq*, 201.

equally critical for the chaplain to speak words that are ecumenical, since the religious beliefs of the soldiers are not often apparent, so as not to offend anyone and to be sensitive to the various forms of spirituality. With the gradual decline of church membership and attendance in the United States, it is crucial for chaplains to be aware that some soldiers will not identify themselves with a particular faith tradition. Consequently, in order for chaplains to be relevant to all soldiers, the chaplains' words must not be exclusively religious or exclusively from any one tradition. Theologically speaking, we must assert that God is in and beyond any religion and faith tradition.

Chaplains provide pastoral care and counseling to soldiers who may express some difficulty in the task of killing. Unfortunately, the reality of war is that killing will occur. Often soldiers have to kill people directly and/or indirectly. The Iraq War was uniquely an urban war, involving more hand-to-hand combat than in the recent past, a kind of encounter that has not been experienced by most of our technologically sophisticated soldiers. This means that many of the soldiers come in close proximity to their enemy, rather than only seeing them from a distance, such as on a computer screen, or not at all, as when dropping a bomb from an airplane. Soldiers often seek military chaplains before, during, and after killing people, if they have difficulty in discussing the experience. Navy chaplain Marc Diconti describes such an encounter with a soldier: "One of our young Marines was forced to fire on an insurgent who raised an AK-47 on him, and in killing the insurgent, the bullets continued on to hit and kill a nine-year-old girl... That is something the Marine has to deal with, and it's my job to help him. He'll most likely feel it more when he gets home. It's a lot to put on the mind and soul of young men, but that's a part of war."[21] Pastoral care and counseling can effectively help soldiers deal with the reality of unintentionally killing innocent civilians. All people make mistakes, but in the midst of war the stakes are much higher than in a typical day at the office. When soldiers make mistakes, they and other people can die in a matter of seconds. A component of chaplains' pastoral care and counseling includes hearing soldiers' mistakes, even when mistakenly killing innocent civilians, with tolerant responses that will help to affirm the military mission's complexity and yet accommodate the soldier's ability to continue to achieve the specific mission.

21. McCoy, "Service in the Sand."

Another component of chaplains' pastoral care and counseling involves advising military commanders. Supporting the commander's ability to achieve victory is seen as a critical role of the chaplain. Military commanders make many decisions that directly impact the soldiers, often life or death decisions. Commanders depend on chaplains to listen intently and offer sound counsel in order to sustain, support, and/or enhance the morale and emotional well being of military personnel and their families. The uniqueness of the relationship between a commander and a chaplain is described by a reporter, Rod Dreher: "A chaplain's importance to the morale of combat soldiers is so central that if his courage falters during fighting, commanders must immediately replace him, or risk the collapse of the entire unit. The things soldiers in combat are asked to do and to suffer are so extreme that, in many cases, only a belief that God is with them enables them to endure."[22] Chaplains' pastoral counsel with commanders greatly impacts not only the commanders, but also everyone under the commander's chain of command.

Personal Hazards Confronting Chaplains in Wartime and Combat

General H. Norman Schwarzkopf, former Commander of U.S. Central Command and Coalition Forces said, "It doesn't take a hero to order men into battle. It takes a hero to be one of those men who goes into battle."[23] Reflecting on his days as a U.S. Army chaplain serving in Vietnam, Claude D. Newby wrote, "Even so, as I walked slowly among the massed dead, all laid out in military formation, I kept remembering Christ's declaration: 'Greater love hath no man than this, that a man lay down his life for his friends' (John 15:13). These men had lain down their lives, reluctantly in most cases, but they'd done it. They'd chosen the risks of service to country, squad and buddy over the personal security offered by fleeing to Sweden, Canada or onto the college campus. These grunts 'fought the good fight' (1 Timothy 6:12)."[24] Chaplain Newby's experience with the dead young men helped him minister to other young men he encountered. Newby's religious references appear appropriate in the midst of broken bodies and broken dreams because God's word is needed in the midst of brokenness. War is

22. Dreher, "Ministers of War."
23. Newby, *It Took Heroes*, vii.
24. Ibid., 72.

not easy for anyone. War is not beautiful. The soldier is usually the last person who wants to go to war, knowing what waits for him or her.

It is important to remember that the hazards of combat have an effect on chaplains as well as on any other soldier. Chaplains face many physical dangers and spiritual demands when providing pastoral care and counseling during combat. While military chaplains understand the realities of war and the possibility of death, understanding does not make it easier or less emotional for us to support the soldiers. Some chaplains find that their most difficult role in the midst of war is to facilitate the many funerals needed. As Chaplain Daniel B. Jorgensen put it, "Funerals were the most trying ceremonies experienced by chaplains. They were a constant reminder that airmen lived on the thin line of hazardous duty in battle against the elements and the enemy."[25] Chaplain Jorgensen further notes that "probably Chaplain Robert W. Tindall conducted more graveside services than any other [Army Air Force] chaplain in [World War II] . . .He conducted 2,700 funerals, sometimes as many as 35 or 40 a day."[26]

Unfortunately, similar to other soldiers, some chaplains are wounded or killed in the line of duty. Many chaplains provide pastoral care even when they have personally sustained physical injury. Accounts of chaplains serving with injuries provide insight into the extreme realities of their ministry during combat and war. Some chaplains have been noted for their herculean acts of working while being themselves wounded. For example, during the Spanish-American War, "[Chaplain Swift] was recommended for the Medal of Honor for his bravery during the battle of San Juan. During the fighting, and for some days afterward, he "worked unceasingly" at a field dressing station, caring for the wounded, reading the burial service over the dead, and assisting with the digging of graves. The station was constantly under fire; the assistant was killed, and several men, including Chaplain Swift, were wounded. The chaplain's wound, however, which was in the leg, was slight, and he continued his ministrations until all the wounded had been evacuated."[27] In the civilian world, unlike the world of military chaplains, a physically wounded pastoral caregiver attempting to provide pastoral care and counseling would be sent home immediately or to a medical facility to receive care, making their personal care the primary

25. Jorgensen, *Service of Chaplains*, 188.

26. Ibid., 190.

27. Stover, *Up from Handymen*, 117.

concern. Sometimes, it is forgotten that chaplains need to be encouraged and inspired, similar to the soldiers they serve.

Another hazard for chaplains serving in combat, as compared to civilian clergy, is that chaplains cannot retreat physically or emotionally from the danger in which they serve. In contrast, most civilian pastoral care and counseling practitioners have access to operational guidelines relating to work load and opportunities to set emotional and physical boundaries from those they serve. They can go home, retreat to a different environment to get recharged, or schedule a vacation, to name a few options. However, for the military chaplain on combat duty, having such opportunities to recharge and prevent burnout is a luxury and often unrealistic. Chaplains usually have a difficult time establishing similar limits and finding ways for renewal, because they usually live with the military personnel they serve, in an environment of constant danger. Depending on the locations and accommodations, the chaplains may share the same sleeping quarters with the enlisted and/or other officers with whom they minister. In an ideal situation, chaplains will have private sleeping quarters separate from the enlisted and other officers in order to provide a small but meaningful private space for meditation and renewal. However, situations are not always ideal, especially when it comes to war.

Another hazard chaplains experience in combat is being captured as a prisoner of war. There are not any soldiers who want to become prisoners of war, and some may even choose to hide and find safety away from the enemy to avoid capture. However, if chaplains are captured, the military expects and requires a higher level of accountability. Chaplain Daniel Jorgensen explains: "The Chief of Air Force Chaplains in the 1957 Code of Conduct study stated, 'Chaplains, if captured, should not attempt escape, but should rather stay with the remaining prisoners as long as any remain in captivity.'"[28] While the intent is laudable, this edict puts chaplains in grave danger. Generally, only officers who are considered non-combatants, such as chaplains and physicians, are encouraged to remain with captured soldiers. Since they are protected by the Geneva Convention agreement, they are instructed to continue to help other soldiers who do not meet the Geneva Convention criteria. In any case, chaplains have to muster up the faith and courage to minister to themselves and others while confined as prisoners. This perhaps forgotten area of pastoral service is evidenced by Roy Honeywell: "Few activities by chaplains equaled in pathos or in devo-

28. Jorgensen, *Air Force Chaplains*, 224.

tion those of the American chaplains who were prisoners of war as they sought to comfort and inspire their fellow captives. Several of them were captured in the first place because they remained with the wounded who could not be moved, rather than find safety in retreat."[29] This example highlights the bravery of chaplains, as they risk being captured by the enemy while providing pastoral care to the wounded. This level of self-sacrifice is greatly appreciated by the other prisoners of war and reinforces the commitment of chaplains and soldiers to accomplish the mission. I have met prisoners of war from different conflicts who have described the dedication chaplains displayed to them in those challenging periods of time. I have also met retired chaplains who voluntarily remained a prisoner of war with their soldiers, while risking their own lives, to be with those who needed them most.

Prisoners of war may appreciate the chaplains' presence; however, the positive impact of chaplains on their comrades is realized not only by our military, but also by our adversaries. Chaplains' pastoral care and counseling can be so influential that even our enemies understand the significance. In fact, the influence of a chaplain's presence and any displays of pastoral care and counseling may prompt the enemy to remove chaplains from the general population of prisoners. The following account documents one such instance during the Korean War: "The Reverend Lawrence A. Zellars, a missionary who became a chaplain in 1956, was a POW. He said that at first there was no objection to religious services and that fellow prisoners given new hope organized the camp to improve living conditions. 'It was then that the Communists realized the effect of religion' and separated him from the rest."[30]

Given the extraordinary demands, and in order to prevent burnout, chaplains are sometimes given relatively short deployments to combat situations. Their responsibilities are heavy burdens to bear. Chaplain Herbert L. Bergsma, Command Chaplain of the U.S. Navy, points to this deliberate strategy: "Chaplain Morton [a senior chaplain during the Vietnam War] felt that no chaplain should remain attached to a field hospital in excess of six months. The drain upon the spiritual, physical, and emotional resources of a chaplain providing a crisis ministry for mass casualties created the need for such a change. As combat operations became more frequent and intense

29. Honeywell, *Chaplains of the United States Army.*

30. Jorgensen, *Air Force Chaplains,* 223–24.

during late 1965 and 1966, it became a matter of policy."[31] Like many soldiers, chaplains are typically not eager to go to combat and participate in war. Chaplains should understand and anticipate that they will sometimes feel as if they no longer want to participate in this kind of ministry, which can be agonizing for them. Chaplains can be in great pain or distress while assisting soldiers. The following quotation describes feelings of two unnamed chaplains who served in Vietnam:

> The difficulties of the northern I Corps in early 1967 had the effect of drawing Marines and their chaplains close together, which proved to be a blessing but also a painful situation in the face of the loss of close comrades. The 2d Battalion, 3d Marines lost 77 men dead and hundreds wounded fighting for Hills 881 and 861 near Khe Sanh. The battalion chaplain reflected, "I wanted to quit and leave, just as other combat chaplains must have felt, but we were given the strength to stay through prayer and the knowledge that someone else would have to do my part and his too if I didn't. Another chaplain stated: "I shall miss them, the living and the dead . . . These men were the only true and real values in the war for me."[32]

The quotation draws attention to one chaplain's inner struggle and strength required to complete the mission, and to another's attachment to those who died. Chaplains display various levels of sacrifice and bravery as they serve a vast number of military personnel.

Chaplains personally have experienced unique pastoral care and counseling challenges while serving during the Iraq War, traumatized and haunted by their experience. "Fort Gordon Chaplain Steve Munson fights back tears as he talks about visiting the Tomb of the Unknown Soldier in Arlington, Va., with a group of Iraq War vets. For weeks after returning to the US from duty in Balad, Iraq—a town troops call 'Mortarsville'— Chaplain Dolinger experienced 'overpass effect,' or the subconscious habit of gazing up at bridges in search of grenade-droppers or snipers. While counseling the first wave of troops returning from Iraq in the fall of 2003, Chaplain West says he had to work hard 'not to lose hope.'"[33] He admitted his personal struggle to remain hopeful. Chaplains can lose hope in the military's ability to achieve the mission(s), the ability for the soldiers to not

---

31. Bergsma, *Chaplains with Marines in Vietnam*, 53.

32. Ibid., 139.

33. Jonsson, "Troubled Soldiers Turn to Chaplains for Help."

get wounded, and/or the chaplains' ability to remain renewed, rejuvenated, and reenergized in order to inspire their soldiers. Chaplains work hard to maintain hope by conducting spiritual practices alone in private, taking moments to rest, and/or to remember the importance of the U.S. military. Chaplains usually have to provide pastoral care and counseling in the midst of hopeless situations and their own personal risk and crises.

Roger Benimoff, an active duty Army chaplain, wrote a book about his deployment to the Iraq War. Chaplain Benimoff shares his personal story and the joys and concerns he and his family experienced in relation to the war. Among his many combat experiences in the Iraq War, he describes a specific incident involving a reservist: " . . . I heard what sounded like a huge blast. . . . I had seen gunshot victims before in my hospital days, but nothing like this. There must have been at least seven bullet holes in his legs . . . We didn't yet know that [Major Brendan Shaw] was a husband and a father, a skilled craftsman and a teacher . . . [and a] National Guards-men . . . the soldiers lost not just an officer, but a leader of their [civilian] community."[34] Chaplain Benimoff describes other experiences under fire, but the previous quote highlights his acknowledgment of reservists' special dual roles in military and civilian life. He admits to being afraid in various combat situations, tired, and challenged by emotional, physical, psychiatric, relational, and spiritual wounds at various times in the process of providing care for soldiers serving in the Iraq War. Frank Wismer, a retired U.S. Army Reserve chaplain deployed to the Iraq War from April 2003 to May 2004, wrote that a deployment to a combat theater is a life-altering experience that significantly impacts the psyche and behavior of those who survive it.[35] Emilio Marrero Jr. would agree with Chaplain Benimoff and Chaplain Wismer. Marrero, a Navy chaplain deployed to the Iraq War twice, describes combat: " . . . death, maiming, destruction, grief, humiliation, hunger, dislocation, finite mortality . . . the need for a community of spiritually focused professionals who care for the soul and spirit of its combatants . . . I joined the Navy to bring people to Jesus as a Baptist but I have come to realize that my greatest testimony to what I believe in and what motivates me in life are not my apologetics but my ability to care.[36] Chaplain Marrero's acknowledgment of the soul's importance in the midst of combat is what my research will continue to explore. Chaplains are the professionals

34. Benimoff and Conant, *Faith under Fire*, 70–74.
35. Wismer, *War in the Garden of Eden*, v.
36. Marrero, *Quiet Reality*, 132–33.

who are primarily responsible for caring for the soul and spirit through the sharing of Scripture and sacred literature, prayers, inspirational devotionals, and the ministry of presence, among other activities in the midst of combat's commotion.

Unfortunately, military chaplains can experience combat situations even within the borders of the United States. Such was the case on November 9, 2009, at Fort Hood Army Base near Killeen, Texas, when U.S. Army Psychiatrist Major Nidal Malik Hassan shot at least forty people, at least eleven of whom died.[37] There are eyewitness accounts of Captain John Gaffaney, 56, a psychiatric nurse Army reservist, who died trying to prevent Major Hassan from harming more people.[38] As expected, chaplains were present to support the military personnel during this tragedy. The Fort Hood shooting drastically altered the course of those chaplains' journey, along with the lives of other people on the base, in addition to many people across the country and possibly the globe, on that tragic day. The words of one chaplain are particularly telling: "'Untangling [our] pain will be challenging,' said Lieutenant Colonel Ira Houck, 56, an Episcopal priest and chaplain for the III Corps who was one of the first on the scene. 'We've been traumatized, too,' he said . . . Houck returned to his house, knelt and prayed, then softly sang 'Amazing Grace' and other hymns until sleep overcame him . . . 'We're all going to remember the people who died in that room,' he said."[39] This is only one way in which a chaplain responded to his own personal trauma. Chaplains will find a variety of ways to deal with combat experiences, even when sharing this experience with other soldiers or chaplains. For example, Chaplain Colonel Edward McCabe responded to the same shooting at Fort Hood in a different manner. "'Total chaos,' he said. 'Everyone's running around. There are pools of blood on the floor and on the walls and on the medical staff uniforms.' While he was there, one of the wounded died, McCabe said. He said a short prayer and used his thumb to place prayer oils on the forehead of Lieutenant Colonel Juanita L. Warman, 55, of the 1908th Medical Company . . . The following evening, when his cellphone finally quieted, he poured himself a few extra snifters of

---

37. Miles, "Obama Pledges Support for Fort Hood Community." The exact numbers have been difficult to determine, because many people were hospitalized and victims' names have not been officially published.

38. Zoroya, "Witnesses Say Reservist Was a Hero at Hood."

39. Jervis, "Chaplains: We Are Traumatized, Too," 3.

cognac. 'That helped,' he said."[40] This serves as one actual example of how chaplains use self care to sustain themselves while providing pastoral care and counseling through combat and war.

Chaplains' Wartime Responsibilities on Home Base

Chaplains have a wide range of responsibilities on their home bases during wartime. In my own case, while serving as an Air Force chaplain reservist with the 927th Air Refueling Wing during 2003–2005 at Selfridge Military Base in Michigan, I was ordered to fly to Washington, DC, to meet and escort an Air Force reservist back to the home base in Michigan to make sure he returned safe and sound. This reservist was returning from the Iraq War ahead of schedule, because emotionally he could no longer handle the combat and war environment. I counseled the troubled airman during our flight. I did not know the soldier prior to this encounter, but he spoke with me candidly as I listened and allowed him to share his experience. I displayed an active, attentive, non-judgmental manner, including eye contact and non-verbal gestures to affirm the reception of the messages he conveyed. The few times I spoke, I offered short questions such as, "How did you feel about that?" "Do you want to say more about that?" and "I am glad you are able to share your story with me." My sense of the soldier's perception of me in my role as chaplain was a combination of gratitude and relief. His willingness to speak freely with me is customary of soldiers' general receptiveness to chaplains because of the familiarity and confidentiality associated with the chaplain's role. When we returned home, I referred him to a variety of local and regional resources. My thoughts and feelings about this experience are that chaplains' pastoral care and counseling are essential during all the stages of pre-deployment, deployment, and post-deployment. I also feel we have a great military organization that recognizes the importance of a pastoral presence for their soldiers.

One of the unique aspects of the military is the sense of camaraderie. As an Air Force chaplain reservist, I have often eulogized soldiers killed in action, presiding over their memorial services held at Riverside National Cemetery. I did not know these soldiers before their deaths. When a soldier's memorial service is announced at any national cemetery, soldiers of any military branch usually attend, regardless of whether they personally knew the fallen one. Soldiers have shared experiences—taking an oath to

40. Ibid.

protect the United States against enemies foreign or domestic, wearing the uniform, and experiencing the various stressors of military life. I make it a point to interact with the deceased soldiers' families before, during, and after the funeral service. Soldiers' families are generally appreciative of a traditional military funeral, because it acknowledges their loved ones' service and sacrifice in an honorable manner. As a chaplain, when I eulogize fallen soldiers I discuss service and sacrifice, because those are two components that constitute the core of our soldiers' duty.

Here I have described the role of the military chaplain in peacetime, in wartime combat, and on the home base during wartime. Next, we will turn our attention to the historical role of the military reserves prior to the Iraq War.

Chapter 3

The Military Reserves
before the Iraq War

A BRIEF HISTORY OF THE MILITARY RESERVES

This chapter will detail the history of the military reserves, emphasizing their role as primarily an immobile organization that generally did not enter international war zones. I intend to lay the groundwork for considering the dramatic changes in the role of the reserves during and after the Iraq War.

After emigrating from England and settling in North America, the colonists considered it necessary to fight for independence from the Kingdom of Great Britain during this period. The earliest forerunner to today's reserves was active during the American Revolution. While the colonies did not have an extensive organized army, they did have citizen-soldiers who could follow orders given by the militia leaders and military strategists of that time. These citizens organized across the country to fight for their independence and were successful in their quest for freedom. During the 1800s, citizen-soldiers and the militia were called upon again to fight in the Civil War. The vast majority of traditional citizen-soldiers and militias transitioned later into seven government-run organizations called the reserves,[1] which were created by all three branches of the U.S. government. The Army

1. Gross, *Air National Guard,* 1–20.

Reserve was established first, in April 1908.[2] The second reserve branch formed was the Navy Reserve on March 3, 1915.[3] The Army National Guard followed in 1916,[4] the Marine Corps Reserve on August 29, 1916,[5] the Coast Guard Reserve on February 19, 1941,[6] and the Air National Guard on September 18, 1947.[7] Finally, the Air Force Reserve was established in 1948.[8] The military guard organizations generally have state missions led primarily by the states' governors. These reserve organizations generally have federal missions. For the purpose of my research, "reserves" and "reservists" signify both guard and reserve organizations. Prior to the initiation of the Iraq War in 2003, these reserve groups focused primarily on matters relating to national affairs or short deployments rather than participating in extended deployments related to wars.

The perception of military reservists before the Iraq War was that they were long-term but part-time personnel who maintained minimal military skills and a state of readiness that would allow them to transition quickly to provide limited support to the country in war time. "Limited support" often was translated as the reserves deploying to humanitarian missions within national boundaries and/or in international settings for a few weeks or a few months at a time. In general, most military leaders did not think the reserves were trained or prepared to enter into international combat and other wartime duties. Military leaders generally believed reservists' service should be restricted to limited roles related to domestic issues. General Curtis LeMay, who gained prominence through his airplanes' bombing tactics in Japan and in Europe during the 1940s and 1950s, became a military legend who rose to the rank of four star general in the U.S. Air Force, and who served as former commander of the Strategic Air Command, among other high profile military and government posts.[9] General LeMay was known to exemplify the attitude of many military commanders toward the reserves. "General LeMay observed that those Air Guard units in Europe . . . could get some planes in the air. How well they could pilot

---

2. U.S. Army Reserve, "History."

3. U.S. Navy Reserve, "Navy Reserve History."

4. Army National Guard, "Legal Basis of the National Guard."

5. U. S. Marine Corps Reserve, *Marine Corps Reserve,* 4.

6. U.S. Coast Guard, "History of the Coast Guard Reserve."

7. Rosenfeld and Gross, *Air National Guard at Sixty,* i.

8. U.S. Air Force Reserve, "Who We Are."

9. Ford, "B-36."

them is something else again . . . it wasn't the kind of outfit that we should have had in the Reserves at that point. They just weren't ready."[10] Many military leaders preferred that if reservists were deployed in a time of war, they would be used only to provide operational support in areas far away from the battle lines. Before the Iraq War, these were not the only restrictions some people wanted to place on the reserves, as reported by Charles Gross, Chief of the Air National Guard history program in the National Guard Bureau: "Missions such as nuclear deterrence, which require extremely high state of readiness, intense operating tempos, and frequent deployments, are usually not considered appropriate for the Guard."[11] High-level political leaders have often agreed with military leaders regarding prohibitions against deploying reserve personnel into combat and war zones, especially in international matters. However, these leaders often had different reasons for not wanting the reserves involved in combat and war zones. Military concern over reserve deployment usually related to issues of readiness and/or capability, but politicians' concerns were usually related to public opinion. The popularity of a war and/or the potential impact of a war on voters influenced the way political leaders chose to use reservists. President Lyndon Johnson decided not to include the reserves in the Vietnam War. Lewis Sorley explains:

> Lyndon Johnson astounded the defense establishment by his refusal to call the reserves to support expansion of the war in Vietnam, perhaps the most fateful decision of the entire conflict. Johnson's refusal was apparently motivated in part by reluctance to spread the effects of the war through the population—certainly many more families and virtually every town and city would be affected by a call-up of any proportions, with a much different class cross-section and much greater political impact than draft calls affecting only those who could not engineer a deferment. Another reason for Lyndon Johnson's unwillingness to call up the reserves was the hope that he could prosecute the war on a low-key basis, not really having to go to war big time . . . That ruled out calling the reserves.[12]

Sorley makes a crucial point in addressing the "different class cross-section" as it relates to the draft and the reserves. The Vietnam War draft heavily

10. Gross, *Air National Guard*, 92.

11. Ibid., 173.

12. Sorley, "Creighton Abrams and Active-Reserve Integration," 37–38.

impacted the poor and people of color, who could not easily avoid the military by quickly getting into college, financing a move to another country, or enlisting in the reserves. "Reservists and guardsmen were better connected, better educated, more affluent, and whiter than their peers in the active forces."[13] The wealthier—and often white—segments of the population were significantly more successful in avoiding the draft.

Many people would agree that racial diversity enhances an organization's creativity and productivity, and that today's U.S. military, including the reserves, is somewhat racially diverse; but this was not always the case. It took years of intentional effort to achieve a semblance of racial diversity in the reserves. "Discrimination varied among states, but ten of them with large black populations and understaffed Guard units still had no black Guardsmen in their ranks as late as 1961. Concerned with the situation, in June 1962, President Kennedy appointed a committee headed by Washington, D.C. Attorney Gerhard A. Gesell . . . .The Gesell committee stressed that the National Guard was the only branch of the Armed Forces that has not integrated . . . Effective progress in integrating the Guard, however, would not come until the 1970s."[14]

I entered the Air Force Chaplain Candidate Program in 2000 while a master of divinity student at Duke University Divinity School. The Air Force Chaplain Candidate Program is a means by which students preparing for religious leadership can evaluate their compatibility and potential for commissioning as an Air Force chaplain.[15] All military chaplain candidate programs are designed to allow students pursuing professional religious degrees to acquire experience in military chaplaincy so that they can seriously consider, and be seriously considered, to serve in the reserves and/ or active duty according to the needs of the specific branch of the military. During my ten years serving my country as an Air Force chaplain reservist, it has always been obvious to me that I am a rarity as an African-American chaplain reservist. Hopefully, the reserves and the military overall will continue to make progress toward racial diversity, and other types of diversity within their ranks.[16]

13. Musheno and Ross, *Deployed*, 18.

14. Gross, *Air National Guard*, 101.

15. U.S. Air Force Reserve, "Air Force Command—Chaplain Candidate."

16. Ginsberg, "Review of the Defense Authorization Request," http://armed-services. senate.gov/statemnt/2010/03%20March/Ginsberg%2003-10-10.pdf, 5.

As previously mentioned, President Johnson decided that the reservists would not be deployed overseas during the Vietnam War in the 1960s and 1970s. The active duty troops fighting this war were stretched and encountering incredible barriers to success, as Daniel Ginsberg, Assitant Secretary of the Air Force, indicates: "1) . . . the reserves, they became a refuge for the disaffected, the dissident, and the draft dodger . . . 2) . . . the reserves got little in the way of new or upgraded equipment, or even support for maintaining the equipment they had . . . and 3) . . . the general populace had no stake in it, and hence no motivation to ensure that the sacrifices of those who did serve were in some way validated by the eventual outcome. Perhaps that was the most fateful result of all."[17] Considering that the forerunners of the reserves were the citizen-soldiers who fought successfully in the American Revolution and helped give us the freedom we enjoy today, not allowing the reservists to fight in Vietnam and relying primarily on an active duty military force for national defense marked a significant change.

Historically, the reserves were used for strategic purposes that typically lasted for limited periods of time. Consequently, extended deployments were rare, and had minimal impact on families. The description "weekend warriors" was often applied to reservists. The reserves have now transformed into an operational force, and the active duty branches cannot function without the reserves. Brendan McGarry explains: "Never before has the military used the 'total' all-volunteer force on the kind of sustained basis that is the norm these days. And the reserve component plays a critical role supporting wartime operations abroad . . ..Yet, the heavy reliance on the Guard and reserve to support the wars in Iraq and Afghanistan also has ignited debates about the role as an operational or strategic reserve force."[18] An operational force requires participation in day-to-day operations, a topic that will be further explored in the next chapter. As a strategic force, reservists generally worked one weekend each month, plus a few weeks throughout the year; they were rarely asked to do anything more than this to fulfill their basic military requirements. Before the Iraq War, reservists were expected to focus primarily upon their civilian job responsibilities and give their part-time energy to the reserves. Additionally, they

17. Ginsberg, "Air Force Active, Guard, Reserve and Civilian Personnel" http://armed-services.senate.gov/statemnt/2010/03%20March/Ginsberg%2003-10-10.pdf, 38–39.
18. McGarry, "Two Careers, Two Jobs," 26.

did not spend an extended amount of time out of the country as part of their routine service.

State-level missions of the National Guard consisted primarily of domestic issues, rather than crossing international borders. The reserves were also asked to backfill active duty positions: they would be activated and sent to U.S. military bases while active duty personnel deployed to other countries. Laws were changed in the latter part of the twentieth century to allow reservists to deploy, but still with some restrictions: "A limited presidential call-up authority was requested and approved by Congress in the 1970s authorizing the President to call up some reservists. [In 1999], the President [could] call up as many as 200,000 members of the reserve components for not more than 270 days without declaring a national emergency (Title 10 USC, 1995)."[19] The president has always been restricted regarding the use of reservists, both in terms of number and the length of time these personnel could be deployed. As previously mentioned, however, President George W. Bush's Executive Order 13223, which makes the reserves available for deployment for up to twenty-four months, significantly increases the president's current power to deploy reservists.[20] The huge difference between 270 days and twenty-four months of service is a major factor in what makes the Iraq War a uniquely challenging service for reservists and their families.

Recruitment/Retention Dynamics in the Reserves

Historically, the option to join the reserves voluntarily, rather than be drafted involuntarily for armed military service in active duty status, offered an element of control over one's life with regard to the choice of armed service. Avoiding the draft was a compelling incentive for joining. The draft did not impact college students, reservists, and people who for other reasons were looked upon favorably by the draft board. As a result, people who had the privilege to be enrolled in college, become a reservist, or have good relations with the draft board members in their geographical location, did not have to worry about being drafted. Gross notes that discontinuation of the draft led to a loss of incentive for enlistment in the reserves.[21]

The dilemma of the reserves' recruitment and retention would become further complicated for reasons that would include not only draft issues,

19. Ibid., 14.
20. Bush, Executive Order 13223.
21. Gross, *Air National Guard*, 128.

but also deployments and differences of opinion pertaining to the reserves' mission and politics. Not only would some people resist mandatory armed service, but they would be more resistant to mandatory armed service that consisted of deployments to countries they believed we were fighting against for unethical and/or unjustified reasons. Fortunately, according to the U.S. Selective Service System, the current rules of engagement are structured to be more equitable for all citizens if the draft were to come into effect today: "There would be fewer reasons to excuse a man from service. Under the current draft law, a college student can have his induction postponed only until the end of the current semester. A senior can be postponed until the end of the academic year. If a draft were held today, local boards would better represent the communities they serve. The changes in the new draft law made in 1971 included the provision that membership on the boards was required to be as representative as possible of the racial and national origin of registrants in the area served by the board."[22]

Only time can tell if the United States will enforce another draft. Some reservists and their families have informed me that they feel as if the reserves have been drafted into the Iraq War, because of their involvement in combat operations in the Iraq War. At any rate, historically, many active duty members did not hesitate to reenlist and/or transfer to the reserves from their active duty service. Before the Iraq War, military leaders assumed that when additional personnel were needed in crisis situations, they could easily request voluntary short deployments from reservists, and that sufficient numbers of reservists would volunteer so that government directives for mandatory mobilization would not be needed. Gross notes the low number of mobilizations in the history of the reserves: "Except for a few major crises, such as Korea, Berlin, and the Pueblo incident, volunteerism, not mobilization, emerged as the preferred method of gaining access to Guardsmen for active service."[23] Before the Iraq War, the few major crises experienced by the United States did not require thousands of reservists to go into combat and war, much less to do so in multiple deployments.

Another factor that directly influences attitudes toward the reserves is the perception of it by civilian employers. Support by civilian employer(s)—willingness to keep reservists on their payrolls during employees' service in the reserves—has a positive impact on recruitment and retention in the reserves. Before the Iraq War, many employers expected their employee(s)

22. U.S. Selective Service System, "Draft Policy Revision."
23. Gross, *Air National Guard*, 77.

serving in the reserves to be away only for limited periods of time. The following describes typical civilian employers' attitudes and expectations before the Iraq War: "Results from a 1996 Air Force Reserve employer survey . . . included 1,318 responses. The survey found that 1) 62 to 64 percent of the employers believed reservists should serve as long as necessary during domestic emergencies, 2) 57 percent of the employers believed reservists should serve as long as necessary during regional conflicts, and 3) absences of 14 to 30 days were tolerable for the majority of employers."[24] People will be reluctant to join the reserves if their military commitment endangers their civilian work due to inadequate support by their civilian employers. Employers can make it difficult for reservists by not protecting the reservists' jobs while they are deployed. Conflict often arises when employers perceive their employees' deployment(s) as having a negative impact on their business. According to the 1996 Air Force Reserve employer survey, the employers believed deployments consisting of fourteen to thirty days were tolerable. Did those employers change their minds in 2006 when some of their reservists deployed for 365 days? I would argue that many reservists had difficulty maintaining their civilian employment, because of their deployment to the Iraq War.[25]

To aid recruitment and retention, the reserves now offer a variety of unprecedented incentives to entice individuals to enlist. The Army Reserve, Navy Reserve, Army National Guard, Coast Guard Reserve, and Air Force Reserve currently offer cash bonuses of up to $20,000 to join their ranks.[26] The Marine Corps Reserve and Air National Guard currently offer bonuses of up to $5,000 for educational purposes.[27] Many of these types of signing bonuses did not exist before the Iraq War; they became necessary to recruit people to enlist in the reserves during the Iraq War. However, it is important to note a 1996 research study's summary conclusion regarding the greatest factors for sustained recruitment and retention in the reserves:

24. U.S. General Accounting Office, *Reserve Forces*, 30.

25. Congressional Budget Office, "Effects of Reserve Call-Ups on Civilian Employers."

26. "Army Reserve Recruiting," http://www.goarmy.com/reserve/nps/money.jsp; "Navy Reserve Recruiting," http://www.military.com/recruiting/bonus-center/resources/navy-reserve-enlistment-bonus-program; "National Guard Recruiting," http://www.nationalguard.com/benefits/bonuses-incentives; "Coast Guard Recruiting," http://www.uscg.mil/Reserve/docs /pay_benefits/bonus.asp; and "Air Force Reserve Recruiting," http://afreserve.com/.

27. "Marine Reserve Bonuses," http://www.marforres.usmc.mil/join/Bonus.asp; and "Air National Guard Recruiting," http://www.goang.com/Benefits?tab=4.

"love for one's country, camaraderie, taste for military life, and communitarianism appear to motivate reservists to continue in the service."[28]

At the time I enlisted in 2000, the incentives included pay while serving a tour of duty during the summer between academic years in graduate school. I took advantage of this opportunity and received money for my tour of duty during the summer at a local Air Force base. Before the Iraq War, it was customary for most of the chaplain candidate programs to offer pay during the summer to their candidates as the primary incentive, without any signing bonuses. Upon my graduation from Duke Divinity School in 2002, I immediately became an Air Force chaplain reservist. Since the Iraq War began, chaplain candidate programs have offered benefits to entice people enrolled in theological education or other religious education—often required for religious leadership in a faith tradition—to enter into military chaplaincy. Currently, the Air Force candidate program offers $4,500 in seminary tuition assistance per year after the first summer of training.[29]

The Army is the largest branch of the military, and to maintain its size, it typically has more aggressive recruiting strategies than the other branches of the military. It takes more effort for the Army to maintain such a large number of military personnel. For example, like the Air Force candidate program, the Army Chaplain Tuition Assistance Program is currently offering up to $4,500 tuition assistance per year in exchange for a four-year commitment in the Army Reserves. But the Army Reserve goes further to recruit chaplains: "The Army Reserve is now offering a bonus of up to $10,000 for ministers entering a USA Reserve Troop Program Unit (TPU) with a six year commitment. The bonus is payable in a lump sum following the completion of the Chaplain Basic Officer Leadership Course (CBOLC), which must be completed within thirty-six months of commissioning." The

28. Lakhani and Fugita, "Reserve/Guard Retention," 123. Division 19 of the American Psychological Association (APA)—The Society for Military Psychology—"encourages research and the application of psychological research to military problems. Members are military psychologists who serve diverse functions in settings including research activities, management, providing mental health services, teaching, consulting, work with Congressional committees, and advising senior military commands. The division presents four annual awards at the APA convention, including the Yerkes Award for contributions to military psychology by a non-psychologist, plus two student awards, one of which is a travel award. Members receive the quarterly journal *Military Psychology* and the newsletter *The Military Psychologist*, published twice a year." See http://www.apa.org/about/division/div19.aspx.

29. U.S. Air Force Reserve, "Air Force Command—Chaplain Candidate."

advertisements to recruit chaplains for the reserves include a fairly aggressive marketing campaign that highlights military chaplaincy in various religious and secular magazines.

The reservists' role is typically not full-time employment. Reservists are full-time when they are deployed, and for this reason, recruitment and retention have specific challenges. Reservists usually have full-time jobs and many other responsibilities while simultaneously serving their country in the military. For instance, I have always had multiple roles while serving as an Air Force chaplain reservist—husband, pastor, graduate student, and volunteer in various organizations. I have always had to seriously consider whether I could manage my civilian schedule to allow me to remain in the reserves. James Griffith describes the reservists' dilemma: "Balancing demands of a civilian job and family life with demands of reserve weekend drill training, extra time spent on unit duties, and annual training . . . Indeed, these competing demands have been used to explain the high personnel attrition of the army reserve. This interpretation views reserve service as secondary to primary commitments of the civilian job and family responsibilities."[30] As is true in most large and complex organizations, retention is an important aspect of the advancement of the reserves. I have personally known several friends and colleagues who decided to discontinue their service in the reserves because it was interfering with their family life, civilian profession, or both.

In most major cities across the United States, a person can easily find military recruiter offices. The role of the recruiter is to help a person transition to active duty or to the reserves within their respective branch of military. Over the past five years, I have observed a steady flow of new recruits enter the Air Force Reserves, joining my current military unit. Generally, every duty weekend twice a month, we intake between ten and twenty Air Force reservists transitioning to our base. Approximately 50 percent of these new military personnel are completely new to the military, rather than transferring from active duty or another branch of the military. Additionally, the weak state of the current U.S. economy is aiding military recruitment. Also, since the Iraq War began, the reserves have become more effective in their recruitment tactics by using demographically targeted television commercials, compelling commercial advertisements played before movies in local theaters, and billboards posted in communities and on major highways.

30. Griffith, "Army Reserve Soldier in Operation Desert Storm," 21.

For example, the deployment of reservists at unprecedented rates is taking students out of college, husbands away from their wives, mothers away from their children, and children away from their parents. Thus, the Navy Reserves has revised their marketing and recruitment theme to describe their changing mission, which includes more flexibility. Force Master Chief Navy Reserve Force Ronney A. Wright writes: " . . . a new guiding principle for the Navy Reserve: 'Ready Now, Anytime, Anywhere' . . . Our Sailors can do nothing without strong family and employer support."[31] "Ready Now, Anytime, Anywhere" is a solid military marketing strategy for national defense. However, it also undermines family life and civilian employment. Too many reserve sailors and other soldiers were deployed to the Iraq War, leaving weakened families and employers, and this only serves to distract and distress the reservists themselves.

Multifaceted Chaplaincy in the Reserves

Before the Iraq War, the military was not intentional regarding the necessity for religious diversity in the chaplain corps. Historically, military chaplains have been almost exclusively Christian clergy. Gardiner H. Shattuck Jr. writes, "Chaplains in the Civil War era not only were almost exclusively Christian, but they were also overwhelmingly Protestant: just one rabbi and approximately forty Roman Catholic priests are known to have served in the Union Army."[32]

In my ten years of military chaplain experience, the three military bases on which I have served have had only Christian chaplains. We had diversity within the Christian faith, chaplains endorsed by various Christian denominations—for example, Baptists, Catholics, Lutherans, United Methodists, and Assemblies of God. However, no religious traditions other than Christianity were represented. Moreover, on all three bases, all the chaplains were male. Currently, special efforts are made to recruit underrepresented religious groups in the chaplain corps. Linda D. Dozaryn reports: "Things have improved somewhat for the estimated 4,000 Muslim service members now on active duty. Two Muslim chaplains serve the Army and two serve the Navy. Along with Hamza Al-Mubarak, two more Muslim chaplain candidates are in training, one for the Air Force and one for the Army. The first permanent Islamic mosque, the Masjid al Da'wah, opened

31. Debbink, "Welcome Aboard," 3.
32. Shattuck, "Faith, Morale, and the Army Chaplain," 107–8.

at Norfolk Navy Base, Va., last November for the estimated 750 Muslim sailors there."[33] The military chaplaincy is trying to create a more religiously diverse corps of chaplains that reflects the religious diversity of the military personnel they serve.[34] Still, currently we can estimate that among the total number of active duty and reserve chaplains—approximately 5000—there are fewer than 150 Catholic chaplains, fewer than sixty Jewish chaplains, and fewer than thirty Muslim chaplains.[35] As one might expect given these statistics, throughout the history of U.S. military chaplaincy, which spans more than two hundred years, the Chief of Chaplains has always been a Christian. To be sufficiently effective, religious diversity among military chaplains needs to be improved significantly, considering that currently there are an estimated 2.5 million people in the military—1.5 million active duty and 1 million guard and reservists.[36]

In May 2002, before the Iraq War began, I graduated with my master of divinity degree from Duke University Divinity School. Upon graduation, I was first assigned as an Air Force chaplain reservist to Pope Air Force Base in Fayetteville, North Carolina. I gained a lot of pastoral experience in this assignment, including pastoral counseling, preaching, and base office visitations. My chaplain candidate peers and I were excited to minister in an assortment of settings across the United States, and we shared a calling to pastoral ministry in the military chaplaincy. Many of us met one another during the Air Force Chaplain Candidate Program, military chaplain conferences, military training, and other military and non-military related events. We assumed that our mission as Air Force chaplain reservists consisted of service exclusively in the United States. Besides, it was common knowledge that *active duty* personnel likely would be assigned overseas only once every ten years in their entire career. Additionally, all of us knew active duty personnel who were never deployed overseas. Our belief as reservists was that we would not be assigned overseas in the long or short term, and especially not to combat and war. This belief was shared by reservists of the previous decade. James Griffith, a former Commander in the Maryland Army National Guard, 29th Light Infantry Division, used

33. Kozaryn, "Muslim Troops."

34. It is difficult to provide religious demographics on military personnel because an increasing number of them label themselves "spiritual" rather than affiliating with a particular religious tradition.

35. Kozaryn, "Muslim Troops."

36. Segal and Segal, "America's Military Population," 3.

a research method that included a questionnaire to survey 30,069 reservists. He discovered the following: " . . . youth joined for the various benefits of reserve service (e.g., bonus money, part-time pay, job training, money for education) without expecting to be called to active duty and serving in combat. In fact, in 1990—less than one year before Desert Storm—80 percent of junior-ranking enlisted soldiers (privates through corporals) in the U.S. Army Reserve said that it was unlikely or uncertain they would be mobilized during their current obligations, normally 6 to 8 years in length."[37] When the Iraq War began in March 2003, however, ideologies and practices began to change in the reserves, especially the role of chaplain reservists during combat and war.

The Iraq War brought a new focus on the significance of interreligious interactions. As it lengthened, chaplains received an increased amount of information concerning interreligious affairs, especially as it relates to Islam. The realities of the Iraq War made it increasingly clear that religion—in this case, Islam—is a major force to be considered, as it affects the military's work. Chaplain George Adams gives details:

> Due to the nature of the ongoing global war on terrorism, certainly the U.S. military will continue to conduct stability operations for the foreseeable future. Since military personnel will have to engage the local population more and more in these operations, chaplains also must be prepared to interact with community religious leaders. Major General Petraeus directed all of the chaplains in his division to make contact with local religious leaders. He saw these leaders as important players in the stabilization of Iraq and viewed chaplains as the natural choice to build relationships with them. In combat or stability operations, many other military personnel will be called upon to interact with the civilian populace, and chaplains must be prepared to do the same.[38]

In previous wars religion and religious personalities were not significant factors, such as they became in the Iraq War. Douglas Johnston, president of the International Center for Religion and Diplomacy, notes: "There have been many instances in which U.S. military chaplains have engaged with local religious leaders in Iraq and Afghanistan in projects ranging from organizing and celebrating community religious services to coordinating mosque renovation projects and forming religious councils. Almost all of

---

37. Griffith, "Army Reserve Soldier in Operation Desert Storm," 196.

38. Adams, *Chaplains as Liaisons*, 13.

these efforts have contributed to improved dialogue, an increase in trust, or a reduction in violence."[39]

Iraq is an Islamic country where clerics have a substantial amount of authority. Religion and religious conflict will continue to be a major factor in Iraq as long as the U.S. military involvement continues.[40] U.S. media will continue to highlight the role of Iraqi Muslim clerics whose authority allows them to influence the involvement of Muslims in war. The influence of local religious leaders on the dynamics of war and combat was not such a significant factor for chaplains prior to the Iraq War. However, chaplains now are grappling with these religious and interreligious issues. John D. Carlson reports on the experience of one chaplain: "Major John Morris, an Army chaplain in the Minnesota National Guard serving in Iraq, commenting on the post-secular complexities of contemporary war: We're in a war. But this is a war where you can't kill enough people to win because this has a spiritual motivation to it . . . That means we have to take seriously religious leaders . . . Do we understand their sacred rituals and rites for dealing with the dead? Do we understand the religious calendar of the area we're operating in and adhere to this?"[41] Major Morris' questions have not been fully answered, but they are aggressively being explored in order to better equip chaplains and the entire military for situations that are similar to the Iraq War as it relates to interreligious dynamics: "The Army has created a new Center for World Religions, which will eventually provide Army chaplains with training on the impact of religion on joint, interagency, intergovernmental, and multinational operations . . . The Air Force and Navy (including the Marine Corps) do not have a similar program, but it is probably only a matter of time before the Army's Center begins providing such training for all of the services.[42]

As an Air Force chaplain reservist, I was sent to Maxwell Air Force Base in Montgomery, Alabama, to enter Air Force Chaplain School in 2000. All reserve and active duty personnel trained side by side. All of the

39. Johnston, "U.S. Military Chaplaincy," 28.

40. This includes situations where the conflict is between local Christians and Muslims. For example, when Christian churches have been bombed, Christian homes invaded, and Christians murdered by Islamic extremists, the U.S. military has had a precarious and important role in providing protection. See "Assaults on Christians in Iraq's Capital Leave 2 Dead," *Los Angeles Times*, December 31, 2010, A6; Parker and Salman, "Christian Priest Faces Grim New Year in Iraq."

41. Carlson. "Cashing in on Religion's Currency?" 52–53.

42. Johnston, "U.S. Military Chaplaincy," 29.

military chaplain schools have now relocated to Fort Jackson Army Base in Columbia, South Carolina, in order to consolidate resources. The geographical realignment of the various military chaplain schools will make it easier for all branches of the military to train their chaplains consistently using similar standards related to interreligious topics.

After reviewing a brief history of citizen-soldiers—from their emergence at the founding of the republic, to the traditional role of the reserves—I highlighted how present-day changes in the identity and expectations of the military reserves, related to the Iraq War, have affected recruitment and retention, and how this war has also affected the identity and expectations of military reserve chaplains. This information now equips us for exploring the significant changes in the kinds of challenges faced by reservists in relation to the Iraq War.

Chapter 4

Military Reservists, Military Reserve Families, and the Iraq War

Stages of Involvement

COMPLEXITIES OF INVOLVEMENT

Drawing attention to the variety of military reservists' involvement with the Iraq War, our discussion now turns, in particular, to various demographics of the reserves and their families in order to better describe the harm inflicted by such participation. The discussion also includes personal accounts of individual reservists who were engaged in this particular war, as well as statements from families, in order to help concretize the numerous complexities of the situation.

Significance of Reservists' Families

Formerly the highest-ranking military official, Admiral Michael Mullen, Chairman of the Joint Chiefs of Staff, knows the significance of reservists' families. As he put it during a speech to the National Guard's Family Program in New Orleans, "military readiness is directly tied to family readiness."[1] Reservists' families are needed to help support and encourage

1. "Joint Chiefs of Staff Chairman: TRICARE Tops Guards, Reserve Families'

their reservist during their service. Similarly, Command Chief Master Sergeant Dwight Badgett of the Air Force Reserve Command conveys the importance of nurturing reservists' family relationships: "Our families are the cornerstone of our existence. Whether our families include spouses, children, parents, grandparents, siblings or significant others, we must provide them with the necessary support to keep all of these relationships happy and healthy. Neglect in this area of our lives can cause tremendous problems with everything else we do. Each of us needs to spend quality time with our families away from our employers and military requirements."[2] In this chapter, which concerns reservists' families, I will describe their physical, emotional, relational, psychiatric, and spiritual challenges in relation to the Iraq War. Later, I will suggest ways to care for them.

The U.S. government has indirectly required reservists' families to engage in the Iraq War. Many of the challenges previously noted about the reservists are true as well about their families: both reservists and their families experienced the same hardships as their active duty colleagues, without many of the resources that are available to active duty personnel. In fact, some have argued that the reservists' families have suffered additional stressors, compared to their active duty family counterparts. "Guard and Reserve families may actually be more vulnerable than families of active military because of having less military experience and less exposure to combat. For families of Reserve and National Guard members, the experience of separation during deployment in time of war differs from active military in a major way."[3] Reporter David Crary describes another aspect of the burden on the families of reservists who are serving in the Iraq War: "If the burden sounds heavier than what families bore in the longest wars of the 20th century—World War II and Vietnam—that's because it is, at least in some ways. What makes today's wars distinctive is the deployment pattern—two, three, sometimes four overseas stints of 12 or 15 months. In the past, that kind of schedule was virtually unheard of."[4] Daryl S. Paulson, a Vietnamese-language interpreter with the 1st Marine Division during the Vietnam War who was awarded the Combat Action Ribbon, and Stanley Krippner, professor of psychology at Saybrook University, comment further: "Vast and unprecedented deployment of reservists has

---

Concerns."

2. Badgett, "Preserving the Reserve Triad," 3.
3. Lapp et al., "Stress and Coping," 46–47.
4. Crary, "As Wars Lengthen."

compromised the stability of intimate relationships with their partners and children, who experience loneliness, role overloads, gender shifts, financial concerns, changes in community support, and frustration with the military bureaucracy.[5]

Despite these unprecedented conditions for reservist families, as compared to active duty families, the military and other researchers have given less attention to reservist families.[6] The lack of research in this area is disheartening, because of the crucial role the reserves and their families have played in the Iraq War. The minimal information we have about what happens to reservists' families, coupled with their lack of support, during the unique circumstances of the Iraq War, have contributed to their suffering and further hinder efforts to resolve or manage their problems.

Harm

It is important to explain the human harm which results from this war, in order to focus on the crucial role of chaplains and pastors to help heal those affected. One individual voice critical to this discussion is that of Karen M. Pavlicin, military spouse of an active duty marine who was deployed to the Iraq War, and who has written a book based on her experience. In *Surviving Deployment: A Guide for Military Families*, she describes three phases—anticipating deployment, living through it, and life after the soldier has returned.[7]

- Phase I, Pre-deployment/Preparation: Stage 1: shock/denial/anger; Stage 2: anticipation of loss; Stage 3: emotional detachment

- Phase II, Deployment/Separation: Stage 4: disorientation/depression; Stage 5: adaptation; Stage 6: anticipation of homecoming

- Phase III, Post-deployment/Homecoming/Reunion: Stage 7: honeymoon; Stage 8: reintegration

Though Pavlicin and her husband are not a reservist family, and her attention is not primarily directed to the reservist community, I will use her framework to organize our discussion of the experience of the reservists and, later, that of their families. This will clearly reveal the essential similarities and differences between the experience of reservists and active duty

5. Paulson and Krippner, *Haunted by Combat*, 18.

6. Lapp et al., "Stress and Coping," 46–47.

7. Pavlicin, *Surviving Deployment*, 6.

soldiers and between the experience of reservists and their families. This comparison is a crucial dimension of awareness for chaplains and pastors as we consider how best to offer soul care to reservists and their families affected by the Iraq War. At the end of each phase, I add a section dedicated to spiritual dynamics and issues.

The lack of attention and research also results in the spouses and children on the home front being largely invisible to our collective consciousness.[8] Reservists' families are residents of our communities who often go unrecognized as being affected by war, even though many people may come into contact with them daily. The number of affected family members is staggering. One report estimates there are 846,248 reservists, related to 1,121,868 immediate family members.[9] Statistics report 403,411 reservists' spouses[10] and 715,613 reservists' children.[11]

Using our limited resources and relying on my experience with reservist families, I will describe the range of problems experienced by these families in relationship to their reservists' deployment to the Iraq War. We will again see the usefulness of Karen M. Pavlicin's framework, which was developed through her own experience as an active duty soldier's spouse, as we seek to understand the challenges faced by reservist families.[12]

In addition to all of the "normal" life stresses, reservists' families also encounter additional stressors, especially during war. As is true for their reservists, families find that no one phase is easier than another—all have their particular challenges. Reservists' families may be immersed in the challenges of more than one stage simultaneously or encounter these stages in a different sequence.

We must understand the people who volunteer their time and energy to serve in the military reserves. Often the service of reservists goes unnoticed in many of our civilian communities because they typically do not wear the uniform while in their local communities. They are also often overlooked in professional circles; despite the extent of their service, there has been no exhaustive analysis of reservists and the Iraq War. For example, in *How Deployments Affect Service Members,* the authors comment: "Finally, many of

8. Lapp et al., "Stress and Coping," 45–46.

9. U.S. Dept. of Defense, Office of the Deputy Under Secretary of Defense, "Demographics 2008," 107.

10. Ibid., 114.

11. Ibid., 119.

12. Pavlicin, *Surviving Deployment,* 6.

our findings and suggestions are likely to be relevant to the Reserve forces. The effect of deployments on Reservists—on their expectations of the frequency, duration, and type of deployments; on the stress of separation from their civilian lives; on their jobs, career, and schooling; on their willingness to continue in service; and on their net pay gain or loss—deserves separate study. The issues and insights from our study may be applicable."[13] A more accurate title for this book would be *How Deployments Affect Active Duty Service Members*, since it does not include a study of reserve forces. Despite the fact that the reserves have given sacrificial service in Iraq and Afghanistan (places of deployment that the authors discuss in detail), and despite correctly noting that reserve forces are affected by deployments in ways very similar to active duty forces, the authors did not include reserve forces in their research and discussion. This is but one example of the reality that the reserves are not given adequate attention relative to their sacrificial military service. Reserve forces deserve a deliberate, focused assessment of both the similarities and the differences of their experiences as compared to those of active duty forces.

Demographics and Statistics

The demographics of citizen-soldiers can offer one important means to better understand those who served in the Iraq War. As previously discussed, one demographic similarity among all the reserve branches is that, in terms of race/ethnicity, most reservists are Caucasian. For instance, in 2004, the Navy Reserve was 62.8 percent Caucasian and 37.2 percent minority.[14] The Army Reserve is the largest branch of all reserve units, and it also has the largest percentage of minorities, yet in 2004 it also was dominated by 59.3 percent Caucasians as compared to 22 percent African American, 12.5 percent Hispanic, and 3.5 percent Asian.[15] The ethnic demographics in the other branches, as of 2010, are as follows: the Air Force Reserve was 73 percent Caucasian, 16 percent African American, 9 percent Hispanic, and 4 percent Asian/Indian/Pacific Islander;[16] the Air National Guard was 79.4 percent Caucasian, 8.3 percent African

13. Hosek, Kavanagh, and Miller, *How Deployments Affect Service Members*, 95.
14. U.S. Dept. of the Navy, "FY 04 Profile," 1.
15. U.S. Army, "FY 04 Profile," 28.
16. U.S. Air Force Reserve SNAPSHOT, 1.

American, 5.5 percent Hispanic, 6.8 percent Other;[17] the Coast Guard is 77.4 percent Caucasian, 5.6 percent African American, 11 percent Hispanic/Latino, and 5 percent Multiple Race.[18]

The military reserves are a fair representation of the ethnic demographics in the United States, with the largest ethnic group being Caucasians, followed by either African Americans or Hispanics, depending on the particular branch of service. Though the reserves are predominantly Caucasian, it is important to note that the number of Hispanics serving in the reserves is increasing. "Hispanic representation also has increased in the military Reserve Components, which have been more active in the current war in Iraq than at any time since World War II . . . Hispanic representation in the reserves enlisted force increased from 7.7 percent in 1999 to 9.2 percent in 2005 . . . Hispanics are more likely to complete boot camp, finish their military service, and to reenlist than any other group of Marines. Latinas and Latinos are more highly represented among enlisted personnel in the Marine Corps than in the other reserves."[19] It is important also to observe that the gender demographics in the reserves are not in line with the gender statistics of the U.S. population. For example, the Army Reserve is 76.3 percent male and 23.7 percent female;[20] the Air Force Reserve is 75 percent male and 25 percent female;[21] the Air National Guard is 81.5 percent male and 18.5 percent female;[22] and the Coast Guard is 86.9 percent male and 13.1 percent female.[23]

The military deployment of so many reservists to the Iraq War affects nearly every state and community in the U.S. But not all are equally affected. More than 40 percent of the reserves come from ten states: California, Texas, Pennsylvania, Florida, New York, Ohio, Georgia, Virginia, Illinois, and Alabama.[24] The deployment of reservists to the Iraq War has also disproportionately affected small towns; communities with populations of a few thousand had to accommodate the deployment of a significant number

17. U.S. Air National Guard SNAPSHOT, 2010, 1.

18. U.S. Coast Guard SNAPSHOT, 2010, 1.

19. Segal and Segal, "Latinos Claim Larger Share," 4.

20. U.S. Dept. of the Navy, "FY 04 Profile," 28.

21. U.S. Air Force Reserve SNAPSHOT, 2010, 1.

22. U.S. Air National Guard SNAPSHOT, 2010, 1.

23. U.S. Coast Guard SNAPSHOT, 2010, 1.

24. Congressional Budget Office, "Effects of Reserve Call-Ups on Civilian Employers," 5.

of reservists, for long periods and/or multiple times. In too many cases, these deployments devastated families, employers, and the communities at large.

An example can bring the impact of these statistics and generalities to life. As a chaplain reservist, I gave an invocation at a squadron Christmas party in December 2010. During the social activity, one of the reservists, a young man who was about thirty years old, informed me he was preparing to deploy to Iraq for seven months, and it would be his fourth time going to that particular war in the past three years. He asked me to say a prayer for him. The Iraq War officially ended in August 2010, but we continue to send our soldiers to that region, including our reservists, some of whom suffer injury or death. With the harsh realities of the Iraq War in my mind and weighing heavy on my heart, I placed one hand on his shoulder and said a prayer asking God to protect this reservist and to allow him a safe return home.

PHASE I: PRE-DEPLOYMENT AND PREPARATION

To expand on the story mentioned above, if the reservist and I had been active duty soldiers, we would have most likely lived on the military base or in close proximity to the base that we were attached to. We could have had a series of counseling sessions in preparation for our deployment. We would have most likely attended the same weekly Sunday chapel services and participated in many of the chapel programs. Our families would probably have been friends. However, we are reservists; we live in different states, with civilian responsibilities demanding our energy, time, and resources, making it difficult to schedule recurring meetings or appointments. Therefore, all I could do for this reservist was to recommend a few local, regional and national organizations that could assist him. I could only hope that a civilian pastor and/or a faith community in his home town were aware of his military commitment and were there to support him with prayerful assistance as he prepared to deploy into harm's way for the fourth time. Pre-deployment and Preparation in Phase I is generally one of the shortest phases for reservists and typically lasts about seven months. This pre-deployment phase presents specific challenges, not only to reservists but to their families as well.

The reservists' families go through a wide range of moods and reactions during pre-deployment, even before the reservist leaves home. They may never wear a military uniform, but they endure emotional wounds caused by the Iraq War. The Iraq War has posed challenges never before encountered by reservists' families: "Although the military praises the re-siliency that enables most families to endure, some military officials and therapists acknowledge that the wars in Iraq and Afghanistan expose soldiers and their loved ones to unprecedented stresses."[25] These unprec-edented stressors include physical, emotional, relational, psychiatric, and spiritual challenges. During the pre-deployment stage, reservists' families will typically experience shock, denial, and anger; anticipation of loss; and emotional detachment.

Stage 1: Shock, Denial, and Anger

Reservists can experience feelings of shock, denial, and anger in response to the news that their deployment is imminent. These reactions stem largely from the fact that most reservists never anticipated deployment. When they realize there is very little they can do to loosen the military's influence upon their lives, they are often shocked. Professors Michael Musheno and Susan M. Ross highlight the reservists' dilemma: "Their lives are no longer their own. The nearly fifty years of the Reserve as the home of America's weekend warriors has come to an abrupt end. They are now the new conscripts of the twenty-first-century U.S. Army."[26] Surprisingly, Musheno and Ross charac-terize reservists as "the new conscripts," or draftees. Reservists frequently experience anger over the feeling that they have been drafted into the Iraq War against their will. "As military reservists continue to constitute nearly 40 percent of the 150,000 U.S. forces now deployed in Iraq, public debate continues to grow about the military's current reliance on the reserves. Some analysts have even called the military's consideration of extended call-ups for reservists part of a 'back-door' draft."[27] Ironically, *active duty* soldiers were not automatically deployed to the Iraq War; their deployment is based upon a system that considers a soldier's expertise, geographical location, and other variables. There are instances when active duty soldiers are not deployed to Iraq, while reservists are sent to Iraq multiple times. Many reservists feel that there should be distinctions between their roles and responsibilities and those of their active duty counterparts, in relation

25. Lapp et al., "Stress and Coping," 49.

26. Musheno and Ross, *Deployed*, 14.

27. Segal and Segal, "U.S. Military's Reliance on the Reserves," 1.

to war and combat duty. One reservist who was previously an active duty soldier explains: "I've been deployed twice as a reservist and none as an active member. What's wrong with that picture? That's the end . . . There's people who do this active. I've done [active duty], too, more than willing to—wherever you want me to go, I'll go. Nope? [You haven't deployed me?] Time's up. Wow, I didn't even get nowhere . . . Well, here I am as a reservist, and I get called out twice in two years with a four-month break. Wow, what else is next? Do I go active duty? Maybe I'll have a better chance not getting deployed out."[28] The incredulity in the voice of this soldier, who was first on active duty and is now in the reserves, expresses the infuriating inequity experienced by many reservists regarding deployment.

As an Air Force chaplain reservist, I have observed more instances of shock than of denial and anger in reservists receiving news of deployment. The reservists' shock can manifest itself in disturbing dreams and/ or repeated thoughts of unease about the deployment. I am not suggesting that reservists do not experience denial and anger, but it has been my experience that those emotions are not overwhelming or primary for the majority of reservists. Most reservists cannot afford to allow denial to be their primary feeling or method of operation, knowing they have to convey the reality of their deployment to their family, friends, employers, employees, and other organizations with which they are involved. Furthermore, the majority of reservists do not to allow anger to be their primary feeling, because that can delay, distract, or prevent them from focusing on completing important preparation documentation and training. Time is of the essence during pre-deployment and most reservists know to use it wisely, even while in shock.

One of the unprecedented stressors faced by the families of reservists is not only the possibility of deployment but also its uncertainty. Most of my conversations with reservists' families include the topic of the Iraq War, whether or not their reservist has been deployed. Many of these families were thinking and worried about deployment every day, while awaiting a deployment notice. For most, those particular thoughts provoked angst and sorrow. It was difficult for family members to carry out their routines, wondering when their reservist would be selected to deploy to the Iraq War. The fact is that reservists' families were already feeling the emotional impact of this war.

28. Musheno and Ross, *Deployed*, 71.

Thus, it may be surprising that for most reservist families, the first reaction to the notice of deployment is shock and denial. It takes some time for the family to grasp that the possibility has now become reality, and their family life will soon be altered in a radical way. The families I have met have made comments like the following: "I wish that I could stop thinking about it, and it would just go away and not happen," "I am in too much shock to begin any preparation right now," and "I did not think it was going to happen to us."

As the pending deployment begins to feel more real, it is not unusual for some members of the family to experience anger—manifested at different times and to different degrees—directed at the war effort, the military, their reservist, or even God. In most cases, when a family member joined the reserves, deployment to Iraq was not expected to be part of their duties.

In the midst of their shock, the reservists' families can experience various challenges, which commonly might include physical problems such as high blood pressure or sleeplessness, and emotional or psychiatric problems such as depression, anxiety, or other mood disorders. Eventually, though, the spouse, children, and other family members typically try their best to enjoy the remaining time with the reservist in the midst of these uncomfortable emotions, before he or she deploys.

Stage 2: Anticipation of Loss

Pre-deployment, reservists are coming to terms with a wide range of serious potential losses related to their service in the Iraq War. Most significantly, they are anticipating a life-altering injury or death. Though the denial mentioned in the previous section protects some reservists from much consciousness of this possible loss, the reality of the dangers of combat takes its toll even when they are not consciously considered.

Reservists also must come to terms with the possible loss of relationship with their loved ones. They are challenged by having to say farewell to their families for an extended period of time. Again, most reservists have at least in the back of their minds the awareness that, in the event of their death, these farewells are their last moments with their loved ones. Additionally, the loss of everyday interactions with their loved ones is daunting.

The reservist families also experience anticipation of loss, which brings them closer to the pending reality of deployment. During this stage, difficult topics are often discussed, such as adjustments of parental roles and spousal responsibilities, and the possibility of injury or death. The anticipation of loss might also lead to other serious conversations between the reservists and their families, and often with an attorney, employer, life insurance agent and/or funeral home director. It is during this stage that the reservists and their families usually try to spend extra time together if their schedules and finances allow.

It is also at this stage that reservists' families more actively anticipate losing a parent, child, sibling, spouse, lover, or protector, among many other meaningful roles, for a substantial period of time. Negative thoughts can flood their minds, or an overwhelming fear, which can lead to a loss of focus—for children at school or adults at work. Many families become nervous, because their family system and its routines are going to be totally (and perhaps permanently) altered. Reservists' children typically do not have teachers or peers who understand their military-related circumstances in relation to the Iraq War. Similarly, adult family members typically do not have colleagues at work who understand their military-related circumstances in relation to the Iraq War. Reservists' families living in small towns are especially vulnerable because of a lack of resources, people, and organizations whose mission is to help reservists' families. Surprisingly, many families who live in major cities also have informed me that they, too, feel isolated, with minimal assistance available for them.

As significant as the loss of everyday interactions with loved ones can be, the reservists experience the loss of connection with other aspects of their civilian lives as well and, if they are employed, another significant loss has to do with possibly leaving their employer. Unlike those on active duty, reservists' pre-deployment process consists of negotiating leave from a civilian employer and other civilian responsibilities, while preparing to enter a military environment for an extended period of time. In many cases, the reservists had dedicated themselves for a lifetime to their work in the civilian world, while also serving in the military. Now, they must anticipate potential losses related to their civilian employment and other roles they had had in their communities. We noted previously that, as the Iraq War progressed and deployments increased in duration and frequency, the security of reservists' civilian employment was threatened. Some reservists experienced decreased salary and benefits, and even the loss of their jobs as employers reassigned their positions to other employees. Further, there was the potential of being unable to return to their civilian employment because of physical and psychiatric injuries due to combat.

Stage 3: Emotional Detachment

Pavlicin describes the third challenge during the pre-deployment phase as emotional detachment. For the reservist, this refers to the affective and relational distance that develops relative to their civilian world, so that they are emotionally able to leave and then enter into the military world for extended periods of time. Put another way, pre-deployment demands that the reservists begin to embrace more completely their military identity and to detach themselves emotionally from their civilian identity, from their families and civilian responsibilities, in order to fully engage their military roles. They need to reduce their personal distractions so as to increase their focus on their role as soldiers.

Active duty service people have the military as their primary vocation, but reservists must grapple with balancing the military as a part-time vocation with their full-time civilian vocation. From this perspective, we can see that emotional detachment is a necessary part of pre-deployment, not only because it can enable a reservist's internal coping but also because reservists are powerless against the military's ability to suddenly redirect their lives. "For the members of the 893rd [Army Reserve Unit], most of whom were already experiencing the competing demands of a variety of family responsibilities and civilian careers, including the pursuit of full-time education, the call to active duty by the military in the face of a national crisis, with few exceptions, trumped all other institutional and personal demands. Once called to involuntary deployment under wartime conditions, many of the reservists, including those with previous active-duty experience, were surprised by the military's grip."[29]

The Iraq War required the military to become increasingly demanding on reservists, directing their energy and time, with little regard to their civilian responsibilities. I have learned that it has always been a general rule that reservists must learn to balance both civilian and military responsibilities in order to function well and accomplish the mission. Furthermore, in order for reservists to fulfill their basic monthly military weekend duty, it is essential for them to let go of their civilian customs, so they can be optimally present for military service. Before their deployment, reservists often have more difficulty in the process of emotional detachment when family members, employers, and/or employees are overwhelmed by their pending

29. Musheno and Ross, *Deployed*, 153.

deployment and remain in the state of denial and anger that Pavlicin notes can be part of Stage 1.

Emotional detachment becomes increasingly difficult when reservists anticipate their future absence during significant events—for example, the birth of a child, a close friend's surgery, a special milestone in their children's lives, or other important responsibilities and goals, such as the maintenance of their homes. At this stage, reservists must now focus on their upcoming military deployment and not be distracted or detoured by their civilian tasks. Time is of the essence. Regardless of how much the reservists have become accustomed to and/or enjoy the comforts of home, they must accept deployment.

Likewise, in this stage, the reservists' families can experience the desire to distance themselves from their reservist in an attempt to prepare themselves for their reservist's absence from home. The family members usually display their emotional detachment in various ways, such as by spending less time with their reservist a few days before deployment, deciding not to accompany their reservist to the base on the day of departure, and concealing their emotions—anger, sadness, resentment—during the last days before the reservist deploys. We can see in the comments of David A. Thompson, a former Navy chaplain, and Darlene Wetterstrom, a Licensed Independent Clinical Social Worker, all three of the pre-deployment stages upon which we have touched: "When a soldier prepares for deployment, life can get a little crazy. Families are sad, angry, and grieving the departure of their soldier and generally feeling bad . . . This often causes a disconnect between a soldier and his or her family and can lay seeds of anger and guilt that take root in the human heart for years to come. It is one of the invisible wounds of war that soldiers and family members carry."[30]

Because the reservists and the military significantly need the families' support for a variety of reasons, it is not good when reservists' families are unable to express their genuine feelings about their reservist's involvement in the Iraq War. Families need safe places where they can speak and safe people with whom they can speak, so that they can release the stressful feelings they are experiencing. I have known reservist families who suffer from such negative consequences: family communication becomes argumentative, and it is difficult to convey other feelings; the children feel their reservist parent is abandoning them; and the family struggles with a lack

---

30. Thompson and Wetterstrom, *Beyond the Yellow Ribbon*, 22.

of details about the deployment. These factors help contribute to families' tendency to emotionally detach from their reservist and the entire military.

Spiritual Life during Pre-deployment

A reservist's spiritual life can be a valuable source of encouragement during pre-deployment, but even in the best circumstances it will be tested. Inevitably, questions and concerns related to the deployment will arise. Spiritual life during pre-deployment may further energize some reservists and their families to pray about their concerns regarding deployment, with hopes for a safe return. However, many experience such challenges as a decreasing or wavering faith in God, a feeling that God "is punishing me," and uncertainty regarding which spiritual practices to exercise for strength and rejuvenation. I have counseled many struggling reservists who asked me to identify God's presence during pre-deployment, because they were having difficulty accomplishing this for themselves.

The faith of reservists' families is similarly tested during this period of time. The possible pride they once felt regarding their reservist's participation in the military will be weathered, and the spiritual storm can include a combination of fear and doubt. Although spiritual life may become further energized as families pray about their concerns and hopes for a safe return, there may also be challenges, such as: a feeling that God is punishing them; deployment equated with death; faith in God decreasing or wavering. Many reservists' families have shared with me the stories of experiencing difficulty praying, because of their anger and shock in response to the deployment notification. Families can be overwhelmed with fear of their reservists' death rather than possessing a substantial amount of confidence in God's protective power. Receiving notification of the deployment, a reservist's family can hold resentment toward God, blaming God and also doubting that their reservist will return without serious wounds and/or alive. Pessimism can overwhelm a family, causing them to overlook God's power; they may focus more on God's condemnation than God's acts of mercy.

In this stage, reservists' spiritual challenges may include becoming overwhelmed by fear rather than being sustained by their faith: fear of being harmed, fear of death, fear of their family falling apart, and/or fear of their family abandoning them. It is during this stage when reservists may find it difficult to exercise spiritual practices—such as attending church, praying, participating in fellowship with other believers, and/or reading sacred scripture—because of their lack of confidence in the relevance of those rituals.

Reservists' and their families' souls may be restless and not be fully present in pre-deployment. They may be preoccupied with worrying about deployment and post-deployment. They may be reluctant to focus on the necessary conversations and important acts of preparation. Some of their souls' restlessness also includes an overwhelming desire to simultaneously complete all three phases of pre-deployment, deployment, and post-deployment. Another spiritual challenge to both reservists and their families is the inability on their own to patiently wait for possible spiritual lessons and/or blessings in the midst of the deployment. This particular spiritual restlessness can hinder the effectiveness of the soul care that is being offered.

PHASE II: DEPLOYMENT AND SEPARATION

Stage 4: Disorientation/Depression

It is during deployment that the experiences of reservists and their families differ the most. This is not to say that there are no similarities. In Phase II, Pavlicin suggests that the first stage during deployment is disorientation and depression, and this is true for most reservists.[31] Typically, shortly after receiving notice of deployment, sometimes even mere hours later, reservists have been flown from their familiar surroundings of home and community into the Iraq War. No amount of pre-deployment preparation can prevent the bewilderment experienced by reservists transported in a matter of hours from the familiarity of home and family to the dangers of combat and war. Chaplain Carey Cash describes the experience of one reservist in his deployment to Iraq. "The young private, a Marine reservist from Trenton, New Jersey, had been called up to active duty with no more than two weeks' notice. He had been at work one day at his civilian job, and in a matter of forty-eight hours, he was mobilized at his reserve center, on his way to the front lines in Iraq. He and his fellow tankers had already seen one of their own killed during the first week of the war, shot by an accidental discharge . . . Only two words came out [of his mouth]: 'I'm

31. Pavlicin, *Surviving Deployment*, 6.

terrified!'"[32] Understandably, after the terror subsides, some reservists react with feelings of depression, especially during rare moments of downtime. As is true for most people, it takes time to adjust to new surroundings. Disorientation is a common feeling for reservists when they first arrive in Iraq; most have experienced life primarily in the civilian world, unlike their active duty colleagues. Therefore, reservists may need more time to adjust to combat environments. Upon their initial entrance into the Iraq War, disorientation and depression were two closely linked emotions reservists had to grapple with and get under control quickly.

Meanwhile, for most families, no matter how thorough the preparation during pre-deployment, the reality of their reservist's departure is also disorienting and often may lead to depression. This stage does not have a specific time line; at any given time during the three stages, families may return to this stage. Their family member's actual departure is shocking. Some reservists' families never anticipate deployment, but when it happens they experience at a new level the military's hold upon their lives; many feel despair over their lack of control. They often become emotionally overwhelmed at the uncertainty ahead. I talk with numerous reservists' families who are frustrated about the timing and length of deployments.

Families may discontinue their regular routine of going to school and/or work for some time while their reservist is deployed. Some family members have informed me they have stayed in bed for days after deployment of their reservist, struggling with depression. They felt they could not continue their civilian obligations knowing their reservist was deployed to Iraq. Children may experience unique disorientation and depression, because they typically "will not experience or understand issues related to their parent's deployment in the same way adults do."[33] Depending on the children's ages, they will not understand the realities of combat, the actual length of a six-month deployment, and a host of other dynamics related to the Iraq War. This should not be surprising, considering that even highly educated adults have difficulty comprehending the war.

Many reservists have informed me that the two major factors that contributed to their disorientation in the Iraq War were the particular geographic region and the combat tempo. They believed Iraq to be the hottest, driest, brownest (as in desert with little vegetation), and most desolate place with the brightest sun they had ever visited. They were ordered to

32. Cash, *Table in the Presence*, 121–22.
33. Levin and Daynard, "'SOFAR' Guide," 4.

wear sun glasses to protect their eyes from the sun. The other factor was the combat tempo, consisting of fourteen hour work shifts, six days a week; this pace was needed to sustain a twenty-four-hour-a-day modern war. They were unable to retreat and recharge their energy for a significant period, because they were always on alert. It can be very depressing to continually feel unsafe and vulnerable for long periods of time in extremely hostile environments. All the reservists said that Iraq was unlike any place they had ever experienced.

Stage 5: Adaptation

Next, reservists experience what Pavlicin described as the second stage of deployment—adaptation. However, as compared to family members, reservists may feel this stage to be even more immediate, with even a sense of relief because, with anticipation over, they can begin to actively adapt and begin coping in this new environment.

Paradoxically, the degree of danger may make their work more meaningful. While their families can only wait and wonder about the welfare of their loved one, the reservists themselves have an active and instrumental role in the experience of deployment. Indeed, an often unexpected and somewhat positive aspect of deployment is that, while deployed, some reservists are able to make a meaningful contribution through the use and continued development of skills acquired in their civilian professions. Reservists across all professions are needed during combat and war. For example, District of Columbia Superior Court Judge Robert Rigsby was able to serve as an Army Reserve judge. His knowledge of federal criminal laws and the Uniform Code of Military Justice enabled him to preside over thirty cases ranging from murder to desertion during his six-month tour in Iraq, Afghanistan, and Kuwait.[34]

Similarly, U.S. Army Reserve Colonel Linda Connelly was, in her civilian life, a professor of nursing at the University of North Florida. A twenty-year veteran of the reserves, she experienced a war zone for the first time. Nonetheless, during her yearlong deployment, her professional expertise gave her the capacity not only to coordinate critical care in battle but also to develop the first-ever Iraqi nurse training program. Colonel Connelly provided clinical instruction to Iraqi nurses, despite vast technological and cultural differences. (For example, because of religiously significant gender

34. Stultz and Schultz, "Army Reserve 2010 Posture Statement," 11.

roles, in Iraqi hospitals nurses cannot take care of patients of the opposite sex). To her credit as a professor and a military leader, two of her former UNF students entered the Army Reserve and, as lieutenants, served under Colonel Connelly in Iraq.[35] Even Colonel Connelly's civilian role as professor has been of immense benefit to the Iraq War, because two of her students became reservists primarily because of her example as a citizen-soldier. A third example can be seen in the contribution of Wyoming Air National Guard Captain Sara Kershaw, who used her professional skills during her deployment to pilot a C-130 aircraft on hundreds of missions, moving 49,000 tons of cargo from the United States to Iraq.[36]

Back home, one of the first challenges faced by families in the adaptation phase is dealing with news about the combat—or a lack of news. On the one hand, there is a profound sense of not knowing what is happening in the life of the deployed reservists: What are their lives like? Are they safe? Are they alive? On the other hand, media reports tend to overwhelm reservists' families, because the increased availability of communication and media contribute to bringing the front lines of battle directly into the home.[37] Often, reporting is done by persons without military experience or expertise about combat in general, or of the Iraq War in particular. Children's exposure to media is of special importance, since they have not yet developed the ability to filter media information about the war. Those caring for children need to be prepared to help children process the war images and other information to which they are exposed. "Because global terrorist attacks and the War in Iraq are portrayed in many media forms, there is a great likelihood that children will be exposed to those images. In light of cognitive differences in children of varying ages, it is important that parenting educators give parents guidance in how to talk with their children about political violence in a developmentally appropriate way."[38] News coverage of the war can be useful and important, but excessive coverage can overload the family with too much information and speculation. Also, media focus on personalities and opinions about the war often divert attention from the facts. However, both fact- and opinion-based media coverage of the war can increase the stress level of family members of any age.

35. Ibid., 22.
36. Vaughn, "Message from the Director of Army National Guard."
37. Chartrand and Siegel, "At War in Iraq and Afghanistan," 1.
38. O'Malley et al., "Children's Reported Communication," 1658.

Often, even the adults in the family may have difficulty dealing with what they see in the media regarding the Iraq War. As a form of self-care, those spouses already experiencing uncontrollable thoughts of worry about their reservist may try to shield themselves from news. "Self-care took yet another form, and that was the conscious effort to buffer oneself from the pressure of too much information . . . This represented an attempt to manage thoughts and feelings by controlling information that was coming into the house."[39] Some reservists' spouses were unable to maintain adequate distance from too much information. They experienced episodes of sadness and crying, anxiety and worry, anger, fear, and numbness;[40] some sought a physician and were given prescriptions for antidepressants and sleeping pills.[41]

Not very long after deployment, the everyday challenges of managing family life in the absence of the reservist present themselves. One cannot overstate how much reservists' families became disrupted when a parent was deployed to the Iraq War. Spouses who remained at the home front often had to care for both themselves and their children as they had to play both parental roles during their reservist spouse's absence. Brad Strumwasser, a physician on active duty during the Iraq War, who was first deployed for twelve months, then extended to fifteen months, discovered: "Common problems spouses had while their loved one was deployed included sleep problems, anxiety, and depression. In addition to dealing with their own feelings, spouses also often bore the brunt of young children who blamed them for their father's absence."[42] Some researchers discovered that the seemingly simple resource of rest was coveted by many reservists' spouses. They heard repeatedly that sleep deprivation was a problem; some spouses had difficulty going to sleep, others had frequent nightmares.[43]

Similar to reservists' spouses, their children also experience a wide range of challenges. Dr. Strumwasser discovered that bedwetting and daytime enuresis were not uncommon among toddlers and preschoolers.[44] Children often became estranged from deployed parents after long absences. Reservists' children were not oblivious to their parents' engagement

39. Lapp et al., "Stress and Coping," 56.
40. Ibid., 57.
41. Ibid., 58.
42. Strumwasser, "Effects of Deployment on the Family," 16.
43. Lapp et al., "Stress and Coping," 56.
44. Strumwasser, "Effects of Deployment on the Family," 17.

in the Iraq War and, similar to adults, the children suffered. In my role as chaplain, I have had conversations and counseling sessions with spouses, parents, and guardians seeking guidance for their teenagers who were rebelling, apparently because one of their parents was deployed to Iraq. For too many children, deployment can be traumatic. "National Child Traumatic Stress Network also states those at risk for stress include youth who have endured multiple deployments, those who do not live close to military communities, and National Guard and Reserve youth. Today's world requires everyone to be engaged with the community of youth who support our Nation's Armed Forces."[45]

The emotional scars of reservists' families are substantial, and their children are among the most affected casualties of the Iraq War, even though they never set one foot in an official combat or war zone. Beyond the everyday challenges faced by all families, deployment during the Iraq War has brought devastation to scores of reservists' families. In some cases, deployment has led to reservists' families or children being geographically relocated. The National Military Family Association describes this poignant dilemma that afflicts reservists' families: "National Guard and Reserve families can be on the move, too. Additionally, children of single service members may have to move in with a grandparent or other relative when their parent deploys. Oftentimes this means changing schools and leaving friends behind."[46] Children of single reservists are especially susceptible to relocation to a different residence during deployment, and their safety is often of most concern.

Deployment has also been devastating for many couples, who have had to cope with readjusting to each other once they are reunited.[47] Couples sometimes experience unbearable strains upon their relationships. As noted previously, the Iraq War has contributed to a substantial number of divorces. Dr. Strumwasser admits that after fifteen months, his Iraq War deployment was over and so was his marriage, as was the case for some of the other soldiers in his unit as well.[48] Ray Nishikawa, Air Force Reserve Command's Airman and Family Readiness Chief, describes special challenges for reservists' families: "Deployments are always going to be a stressful, try-

45. National Military Family Association, "Ten Things Military Teens Want You to Know," 3.

46. Ibid., 8.

47. Thompson and Wetterstrom, *Beyond the Yellow Ribbon*, vii.

48. Strumwasser, "Effects of Deployment on the Family," 17.

ing time for both the person who deploys and for the family members left behind . . . But they can be especially difficult for the families of Reservists because our families don't always have easy access to the counseling and care that are available at all Air Force bases. Still, we owe it to our Air Force Reservists to try and make the deployment process as painless as possible, both for them and their family members."[49] Active duty personnel during the Iraq War have had more institutionalized support, but even their marriages were not immune to divorce.

One unexpected challenge during deployment is that the family unit and home often become more vulnerable to criminal activity. Especially when male reservists are deployed, their families may be targeted for crime. As a chaplain reservist, I encountered a situation with a teenager whose father was deployed. The teen involved himself in gang-related activity that eventually placed the entire family in jeopardy, because the criminals targeted their home. An online program for families of reservists, sponsored by the National Guard, warns explicitly of this danger: "Don't spread the word that your loved one has been deployed. Tell children not to either, and teach them what to say on the phone. Make sure you have a peephole on your front door, and use it. All doors should have deadbolt locks."[50] Many reservists' families, while their reservist is deployed, have little access to military resources. Often, reservists live a distance from a military base; they may not be able to access the counselors, psychiatrists, physicians, and medical centers provided by the military. In fact, the National Military Family Association reports that more than seven hundred thousand National Guard and Reserve children might never live on a military installation.[51] Moreover, those reservist families who manage to access the military's services are generally covered by health insurance only a few months before deployment and a few months after their reservist's deployment. Military insurance coverage, such as Tricare and the Veterans Administration's hospitals, has very specific guidelines regarding care for reservists' families—it is typically available for a limited time and for a (nominal) fee.

Residing a formidable distance from the resources of active duty bases again becomes a serious impediment, since reservists' families generally have less experience with various nuances of military life and do not have

49. Joyner, "Deployment Support," 8.

50. National Guard Family Program, "Learn about Deployment," 11.

51. National Military Family Association, "Ten Things Military Teens Want You to Know," 12.

contact with active duty military families who could help them learn what is available. A spouse whose husband was previously on active duty and is now in the Navy Reserves is in an excellent position to discuss access to services: "I feel with the reserves units there is not enough contact with the command and the family service centers. My husband was on active duty for 10 years and I am aware of the support that is available to them, and the support for reserve families is practically non-existent. It should be more available to them even when they are a great distance from a military installation."[52] The military owes reservists' families the very best support possible. Additionally, the civilian community owes the reservists' families the very best support as well. Over the years, it has been common for me to receive phone calls from reservists' families from around the country, seeking my counsel as an Air Force chaplain reservist. Often family members are so desperate to find a chaplain, they will call several military bases until they find one to speak with, even if the base is far from their home. These families somehow find my number as the chaplain and/or they randomly call the chaplain's office, because they do not have any resources located near their homes to receive care. It quickly becomes apparent to me that too many reservists' families are not in a relationship with pastors or other professionals in local communities who could provide appropriate care.

We can see that in many ways reservist families are isolated. They often have been the only persons, or one of the few in their work setting, neighborhood, or faith community, who have a loved one involved with the Iraq War. Reservists' families seldom have the opportunity to relate to anyone or even know other people who are associated with the Iraq War. Military organizations acknowledge the dilemma of reservists' families: "it's hard not to feel a special empathy for guardmembers and reservists and their families."[53] This lack of relationship contributes to isolating reservists' families from support. These families quickly become painfully aware they are experiencing the Iraq War much differently than their active duty and/or civilian neighbors, coworkers, and other counterparts. "Reservists are 'extremely geographically dispersed, and we live in communities that have very little understanding of . . . what it's like to wear the uniform,' Army Reserve Brig. Gen. Margaret Wilmoth, Assistant for Mobilization and Reserve Affairs for the Office of the Assistant Secretary of Defense for Health Affairs, noted. And their children go to schools with other children 'who

---

52. National Military Family Association, "Report on the Cycles of Deployment," 10.

53. "No Thanks for Your Service," 34–35.

don't know what it's like to have mom, dad, or brother or sister deployed,' she added."[54]

The greatest hardship for families occurs when their reservist is killed. Too many reservists' families have experienced a notification call at their home by the military informing them that their reservist was killed in the Iraq War. The Associated Press has reported that casualties in Iraq have shifted toward citizen-soldiers as their combat role has grown to historic levels.[55] "The National Guard and Reserves are suffering a strikingly higher share of U.S. casualties in Iraq . . . Reservists have accounted for one-quarter of all U.S. deaths since the Iraq war began . . ."[56] I have noticed that reservists' families are generally more disturbed by the death of their reservist than are the civilian members of my church who experience the death of their civilian family members. This may seem odd, because reservists' families are keenly aware of the dangers of war. One may expect the reservists' families to be more prepared for their reservists' possible death but, oddly, this is rarely the case. On average, most civilian families have significant advantages over reservists' families. For example, civilian families are generally in physical proximity to their deceased family member. They usually know where and how their loved one died. Civilian families have some control and decision-making rights not afforded the family of the reservist: civilian families can usually decide when to stop medical treatment for a dying family member; they can choose the funeral home and means of preparing the body; and they usually know where the body is. In contrast, reservist families generally agonize over not knowing the specific circumstances and last details of the life of their deceased reservist. They are dependent on the military's choices in caring for and transporting the body of their loved one. Sometimes their reservist is killed in a combat situation that literally disintegrates the body, and the family has no opportunity to view the remains of the deceased.

Perhaps the greatest similarity between civilian and reservist families occurs when their loved one's death is due to suicide. I previously discussed the reservists' increasing suicide rate. Pastoral theologian Kathleen Greider describes how family members suffer when suicide occurs. For example: "Where persons succeed in committing suicide, it is legal to penalize their families: insurance companies will pay family survivors for death from

---

54. Wilson, "Balancing Act Strains Reservists," 9.

55. Associated Press, "Death Toll Rises for Reservists."

56. Ibid.

homicide, accident, or any other medical condition except suicidality."[57] The suicide rate is increasing in this demographic, and the reservists' families are suffering at a rate as never before. When faith communities respond to suicide as the ultimate sin, that response can add insult to injury as the family members are grieving.

Other Deployment Challenges for Reservists

Despite some similarities, the reservists' deployment is significantly different from their families' experience. Reservists are struggling to do their best to serve the military, while also honoring their commitments at home; these competing commitments typically cause emotional distress.

At the same time, reservists' main preoccupation during deployment is avoiding injury and death—whether their own or that of their fellow soldiers. The death toll for the Iraq War was substantial.[58] Reservists were and are killed in a variety of ways: in action, by friendly fire, by improvised explosive devices (IEDs), suicide, accidents, and diseases. Soldiers can best avoid death by focusing on fighting, surviving, and winning. Thus, ironically, focusing too much on death can become a distraction that not only puts them in more danger but may leave them uninspired and unproductive. The reservists are often witnesses to the deaths of other U.S. soldiers, allied soldiers, insurgents (including members of Al Qaeda), and a wide range of civilians. Chris Plekenpol, a West Point Graduate and Army Officer, describes his experience in the Iraq War: "Before Iraq, I had never seen a real dead person. But within a month of my arrival, I was searching the highway for one of my soldiers . . . I have watched the enemy die and wondered in my heart if it was wrong to witness a man in the moment of his final heartbeat and be glad. I have picked up our own dead more times than I want to remember, questioning secretly why, when I said, 'In the name of Jesus, get up and walk,' nothing happened."[59] Being surrounded by death and the threat of their own death raises many religious, spiritual, and theological questions for soldiers. These types of psycho-spiritual questions and issues can torment soldiers for a lifetime when they go unaddressed.

Those soldiers not killed may still have their bodies permanently impaired by injury. A staggering number of reservists have become physically

---

57. Greider, *Much Madness Is Divinest Sense*, 148.
58. Associated Press, "Death Toll Rises for Reservists."
59. Plekenpol, *Faith in the Fog of War*, 11.

disabled because of their service in the Iraq War. The number of soldiers physically wounded in the Iraq War surpassed thirty thousand as of July 2, 2010, according to the Department of Defense.[60] Generally, most reports do not distinguish between active duty and reservist military personnel who become injured. But it is clear that thousands of reservists were injured physically during the Iraq War.[61] The public is perhaps most aware of the risk of improvised explosive devices (IEDs) that injured thousands of soldiers in the Iraq War; reservists are tasked to spend hours upon hours looking for anything resembling IEDs. Media accounts tend to focus on soldiers who have lost one or more limbs, or who have suffered other physically visible wounds. However, among the most serious physical injuries are some that are not visible, such as traumatic brain injury (TBI), which occurs when a soldier's head is struck due to an explosion, vehicle collision, or other incident. TBI has multiple symptoms that include behavior and/ or mood changes, confusion, chronic headaches, memory loss, and black-outs.[62] TBI can materialize several months after the reservist's involvement in an incident.

The reservists are under physical threat not only from combat itself but from the environment. Native plants and wildlife in Iraq also pose a threat to our soldiers. For example, leishmaniasis is an infectious disease that is originally transmitted to humans when they are bitten by sandflies that have become infected by biting an infected animal.[63] However, reservists are in a more complicated situation with regard to treatment for this threatening disease, as an Under Secretary for Health Information Letter elaborated:

> The impact of leishmaniasis on U.S. military personnel currently deployed to SW Asia has been substantial. Since January 2003, over 600 U.S. troops have been diagnosed with cutaneous leishmaniasis (CL). Several hundred additional soldiers may have been infected. Nearly all cases of CL were acquired in Iraq and were found to be caused by *Leishmania major* . . . CL typically presents as one or more skin sores, papules, or nodules, either painful or painless, with or without a scab, that develop weeks to months after a person is bitten by infected sand flies. In SW Asia, the skin lesions are commonly called "Baghdad boil" . . . While CL is not

60. Available at http://www.defense.gov/news/casualty.pdf.
61. "No Thanks for Your Service," 36.
62. Information is available at http://www.ninds.nih.gov/disorders/tbi/tbi.htm.
63. U.S. Under Secretary for Health, "Guidance," 1.

> life threatening, the skin lesions may take months to years to heal
> and can result in permanent scarring. *NOTE: Health care person-*
> *nel need to focus on the possibility of leishmaniasis in slowly- or*
> *non-resolving skin lesions among soldiers redeploying from Iraq and*
> *Afghanistan.*[64]

Since it takes months for symptoms to emerge, reservists are at risk of not
receiving the proper diagnosis and treatment either before or after they
return to their homes. Treatment can be best provided on a military base or
military medical facility such as a veterans hospital, where medical personnel are familiar with the symptoms and diagnosis. However, there are still
many unknown facts about this disease, such as the range of communicabil-
ity and the degree of infectiousness. Unfortunately, veterans hospitals can
be located more than four hours away from home for the typical military
reservist. While a certain strand of leishmaniasis can actually prove deadly
to its victims when contracted, it does not meet the criteria to prevent soldiers from being redeployed. The Under Secretary for Health Information
Letter further notes: "Visceral Leishmaniasis (VL), also known as kala-azar,
is typically a more severe disease than cutaneous infection . . . The most
common manifestations of VL (fever, weight loss, and an enlargement of
the spleen and liver, and anemia) characteristically develop months, but
sometimes years, after a person becomes infected . . . Because symptoms
are non-specific and often start after redeployment, there is frequently a
delay in diagnosis of VL. *NOTE: VL needs to be considered in any veteran*
with documented, chronic fever returning from an endemic area."[65] Again,
reservists run into a difficult situation, because this particular form of the
disease may not develop symptoms for years after infection. Reservists can
return to their civilian homes and possibly get sick with leishmaniasis years
after their deployment.

In addition to the threat of death and serious injury while deployed,
reservists at the same time experience relational challenges due to separation and isolation from their civilian community. Being in Iraq has hin-
dered reservists' ability to communicate with and nurture relationships
with their families and other loved ones. Numerous married reservists
encounter marital friction, which in some cases leads to divorce, even before they return from deployment. Paul Rieckhoff, who served as a platoon
leader with the Florida Army National Guard for ten months and went on

64. Ibid., 2.
65. Ibid., 3.

hundreds of combat patrols around Baghdad, observed that, in his platoon of thirty-eight people, eight were divorced while in Iraq or a short time after they returned home.[66] Percentages like this one—21 percent of a platoon experiencing divorce during or after service—suggest the extent of the problem.

As noted above, reservists' spiritual well-being is also under siege during deployment in Iraq. One common theme in the military with spiritual significance is sacrifice. At least in combat settings, sacrifice generally describes an experience that includes pain, the giving of something at one's own personal expense, and an unpleasant or not ideal scenario. The use of a "total force" policy to compel reservists' service is characterized as sacrifice: "The wars in Afghanistan and Iraq have required extended deployments of reserve combat and combat support forces, including the call-up of the 893rd Military Police Company. Along with professional soldiers, members of the Reserve and National Guard bear the burden of sacrifice for homeland security, the Iraq War, and the Afghanistan War. While most Americans continue life as normal, catching glimpses of the wars on the TV evening news, the lives of the citizen-soldiers have been taken over by total force policy."[67]

One aspect of this sacrifice is that, at least in many respects, reservists are making the same sacrifice as their active duty counterparts, but without the same job security. "It's hard not to feel a special empathy for guardmembers and reservists and their families, hundreds of thousands of whom have experienced two or three—or more—combat tours in Iraq and Afghanistan since 2001 . . . In effect, they incur similar sacrifices as the regular force without similar rewards. The regular force returns from a combat tour without changing employers but retains continuity under leaders and a career system that value and reward their overseas combat experience."[68]

Another aspect of the psycho-spiritual challenge for reservists making this sacrifice is the perceived nonchalance of U.S. citizens. It is a challenge for reservists to sacrifice for a people who seem to be unappreciative and even unaware of the sacrificial activities required of those serving in Iraq. Reservists sacrifice with full knowledge of public attitudes toward military action in Iraq. They experience a variety of emotions when they make this

66. Shane, "Flood of Troubled Soldiers."

67. Musheno and Ross, *Deployed*, 24.

68. "No Thanks for Your Service," 34–35.

sacrifice, and yet large numbers of people in the United States, although they greatly benefit, may not be grateful, invested, or even aware of the soldiers' efforts. There are limits to how much a reservist can sacrifice thanklessly without developing resentment. One reservist articulated this perspective: "I'd have to say that [as] a citizen-soldier, one word to sum it all up is *sacrifice* . . . As a soldier, when you go overseas—or anywhere for that matter, deployed [or] even homeland—you're not there for you. Holy smokes—I wasn't there for me. I was there for the three hundred million American citizens that are sitting in the country sucking on their chocolate milk at night and watching the *Flintstones* on their television."[69]

There is harm done to reservists' spiritual well-being when they are sacrificing in combat and war and simultaneously feeling unacknowledged, unaffirmed, and unrewarded. The domino effect usually turns into unenthusiastic notions of God. I have provided pastoral care and counseling to numerous reservists who felt detached from their faith tradition or from God due to a sense of abandonment in relation to the Iraq War.

I was watching a television news program recently that explained how deployed soldiers in Iraq were losing their homes in the United States to foreclosure. The program highlighted several soldiers who had such experiences. During this broadcast, soldiers provided testimonies to politicians in Washington, DC, about their unfortunate experiences of home foreclosures while they were away fighting for their country. The politicians apologized to the soldiers. At this point, no one really knows how many deployed soldiers' homes were taken away from them. However, we do know a significant number of deployed reservists' homes were foreclosed on, rather than being legally protected by the Service Members Civil Relief Act. Dan K. Thomasson reports on some of the tactics used by banks and other mortgage funders: "It isn't enough to face death and destruction, particularly those who are part-time soldiers called to active duty from the reserves and National Guard units. Now, adding to their worries is the threat of coming home to nothing despite a federal law that is designed to prevent that . . . It seems that Deutsche Bank and a mortgage subsidiary of Morgan Stanley not only violated the relief act, according to a federal judge's rulings, they did so by obstinately making illegal demands of proof that the Michigan National Guardsman was in fact in Iraq, where, of course, he truly was."[70] Soldiers have plenty to grapple with while deployed, while they attempt

69. Musheno and Ross, *Deployed*, 137.

70. Thomasson, "Deployed Troops Should Be Protected."

to protect to the interests of the United States. At a minimum the United States should try to take care of the soldiers and their families; soldiers should not have to worry on the battlefield whether or not their homes are being foreclosed on. Some financial institutions have admitted to their erroneous participation in not supporting deployed soldiers and they seek to correct their past actions. A financial institution's apology to soldiers was included in the *Los Angeles Times*: "At JPMorgan Chase, we recognize what servicemen and women do for our country. Recently, we have fallen short on our commitments to our servicemembers, and we hold ourselves accountable. We are now going the extra mile by launching several new homeownership initiatives for veterans, members of the armed forces, and their families . . . we will not foreclose on any servicemembers while they are actively deployed—no matter what their financial circumstances might be."[71] Almost every institution and person should think seriously about how they can help support deployed soldiers and their families. At the very least, institutions and individuals should try their best not to be a hindrance to them.

Stage 6: Anticipation of Homecoming

Returning to Pavlicin's framework, I now describe how reservists have been challenged by having a variety of feelings about returning home. Some reservists knew they were returning to a troubled or dissolved marriage, angry children, or frustrated employers. If injured, returning home in a disabled condition often severely taints homecoming. I have had many reservists convey to me that going home is not unlike their deployment to Iraq—both deploying and returning home involve great *unknowns*. Just as they did not know how they were going to fit in the Iraq War, they also did not know how they were going to fit back into their home life and communities. Those circumstances frequently caused reservists to become agitated and anxious. In some cases, soldiers can feel more comfort in their ability to adapt to the Iraq War than in their return to their civilian lives. The anticipation of homecoming may entail considerably more effort than reservists want to expend, or have energy to expend.

Most soldiers, especially reservists, do not discuss in detail the difficulties within their anticipation of homecoming; one reason is that they already have too many concerns to worry about during war; another reason

71. J. P. Morgan Chase and Company, "The Way Forward," A7.

is that they may not know their soldier colleagues well enough to feel comfortable expressing their anxieties. Many reservists were deployed to Iraq with a unit consisting of soldiers they had never met before, so they chose to be selective with the information shared. Active duty soldiers are more likely to have been deployed alongside people with whom they have a longer history, so they tend to have more comfort talking with other soldiers about their home life and other aspects of their life circumstances.

Reservists' families also have a variety of distressed emotions even as they look forward to their reservists returning home from deployment. Families know more about their reservist who deployed to the Iraq War than they do about their reservist who is *returning*. Families often anticipate their reservist's various wounds or, at the least, how their reservist may have been changed by the combat experience. In this stage, family members can experience guilt, realizing that they have made necessary adjustments during deployment, perhaps even to the point of actually enjoying themselves in their reservist's absence. A family can also feel unprepared and unequipped when they have been officially informed that their reservist is returning injured. Sometimes families will not be officially informed that their soldiers have been injured, because of the magnitude of the injury, because the injury was undetected, or because the lines of communication were unsuccessfully accessed.

Families have shared their disappointment with me when they believed they did not have the ability or the means to display all the "bells and whistles" for a hero returning home. Most families want to do something special for their reservists' homecoming, but might not have the financial resources, political connections, or wider community to make a big announcement of their reservists' service in relation to the homecoming. Unlike their active duty counterparts, many of these families do not have much assistance or experience in welcoming a soldier home from war.

Spiritual Life During Deployment

When possible, soldiers attend worship services during deployment. Many chaplains have informed me that when they were deployed to Iraq, their chapel teams were very busy conducting multiple worship services with high attendance, in addition to several chapel programs during the week. Nonetheless, problematic spiritual issues remain. While deployed, reservists can experience all the same spiritual challenges that they did before being deployed, along with additional ones: feeling distant from God while in a foreign land and other unfamiliar surroundings; having more faith in military weaponry for protection than faith in God; and turning against themselves and others in unsafe and/or criminal ways.

Numerous soldiers are spiritually tested and battered during war and are in constant need of spiritual renewal. Many reservists informed me they were always glad to visit with the chaplain during their deployment. The two places that soldiers visited the most during the Iraq War were the chapel and the gym. The gym gave careful attention to their physical bodies and the chapel gave careful attention to their souls.

A reality for many people who commit crimes is usually a deficient spiritual component in their lives, triggered by a variety of dismal circumstances, such as war, which can bring out the worst in soldiers. It is expected that many civilized rules and courtesies are dismissed during war among enemies. That does not justify any unnecessary killings of soldiers or civilians who are considered the enemy. Nonetheless, war's harsh conditions can even cause soldiers on the same side to turn against one another. There have been instances of sexual assaults among soldiers on the same side.[72] Unfortunately, such dismal circumstances as can be found in war contribute to criminal behavior.

During this deployment phase, families also can struggle with spiritual isolation and loneliness, which unfortunately can cause them to further distance themselves from the many possibilities of connecting to spiritual revitalization. Reservists' families have informed me they feel abandoned by God. I do not argue with them, but as I listen to their stories, it becomes evident that a major contributing factor of their sense of God's abandonment includes the feeling of being abandoned by people. Sometimes the reservists' families equate people's lack of support with God's perceived absence. The families experience all the same difficulties as in pre-deployment, along with two additional pains: their church or faith community is oblivious to the challenges of reservist deployment, and they are uninspired to attend church, pray, and/or read the Bible or other sacred texts. Such families can easily become spiritually bankrupt when they do not understand how spirituality is relevant to their circumstances. When this occurs,

---

72. Two articles that highlight soldiers' crimes during the Iraq War are: Gibbs, "Sexual Assaults on Female Soldiers"; Isikoff, "Lawsuit Claims Pentagon Turned Blind Eye to Military Rape Victims."

they may place more confidence in secular institutions rather than religious institutions and spiritual practices.

Another spiritual challenge is the possible collapse of the family unit within the same household. This can occur in a number of ways while reservists are deployed: sibling versus sibling, parent versus sibling, and spouse versus spouse, among other family infighting. This particular challenge can be so disturbing that some family members decide to no longer live in the home while their reservist is deployed.

PHASE III: POST-DEPLOYMENT/HOMECOMING/ REUNION

Stage 7: Honeymoon

Pavlicin describes the first portion of post-deployment—Stage 7—as the "honeymoon." Reservists often experience reunions with their loved ones with honeymoon-like bliss. From my observation, however, the honeymoon can be one of the shortest of the eight stages, lasting a few hours, days or, at most, weeks. The honeymoon brings hugs, handshakes, kisses, and possibly a few parties in honor of the reservists. But the parties do not last long. Hugs, kisses, and celebrations last for blissful days or weeks.[73] The media tend to sensationalize stories of the honeymoon stage, capturing on camera intimate moments, embraces and expressions of joy. The chaplain's or pastor's presence is generally not needed or solicited during this stage. If such presence is requested, it is appropriate to give prayerful statements of thanksgiving for the reunion. It is important to keep in mind the honeymoon stage is special; it may be the happiest, but it is also typically the shortest, and not completely free from challenges. Contrary to popular belief, new problems can emerge and can become more devastating than those in the other two phases.

The reservists soon realize that their civilian world has changed since they left for the Iraq War. Everyone has changed, including them. At that point the reservists and their families must find a way to enter the final and often the most difficult stage in this cycle: reintegration.

73. Pavlicin, *Surviving Deployment*, 16.

Stage 8: Reintegration

Historically, Stage 8, reintegration, has been the longest stage. For many soldiers who have returned from war, it has taken years to reintegrate themselves into their civilian lives with a sense of dignity and sanity, if they ever do at all. Even those reservists who return home without serious injury may find reintegration elusive. Because our country needs productive citizens who contribute to its well-being, our reservists returning home need to function the same as—if not better than—they did before deployment. Our country especially does not need reservists becoming unstable members of society, since we are now depending on them to help defend our country. Yet, for reservists who return home—with or without serious injuries—it is an arduous task to make the transition and remain relationally and professionally present for their military and civilian communities.

A countless number of soldiers' families are still struggling to rebuild their lives after participation in World War II, the Korean and Vietnam Wars, and many other combat experiences. At numerous military-related functions that I have attended, families have shared with me how they continue to grapple with challenges from wars their soldiers participated in decades ago. Veterans Administration hospitals all across the United States continue caring for veterans from past wars. The difficulties of reintegration have been heightened in the Iraq War because of its unfamiliar aspects: "The changing nature and complexity of the Iraq War has contributed to reintegration stresses experienced by service members, their spouses and families. The operation in Iraq, a conventional conflict between armies for only a few weeks, became a predominantly guerilla war with no front-line, constant threat and a disguised enemy . . . compounded by extended or open-ended return dates."[74] During deployment, the reservists' families were aware that their loved ones were engaged in a situation unlike any before, and not only in terms of the enemy being disguised. Other unfamiliar situations of danger involved civilian suicide bombers and religion being a significant factor in combat as never before. It did not make it any easier that the Iraq War was often associated with mixed public opinion on the attacks of September 11, 2001, and U.S. dependency on foreign oil; the reservists' families were not unaffected by public debate on such emotional and divisive topics.

74. Uniformed Services University of the Health Sciences, "Courage to Care: Reintegration Roadmap."

Despite the relief of returning, post-deployment is not necessarily any easier than the other two phases. It generally presents a new set of challenges for reservists' families and requires new ways of dealing with the effects of the Iraq War on their lives. Even what may appear simple—the reservist and family reengaging in everyday life—is difficult. The reservist is not fully returned, again disoriented by the sudden transition to such a different environment. Furthermore, the waiting family is unlikely to restrain their need for the reservist to enter back into family life as it was before their soldier's deployment. "[Reservists] returning from military service are often hit right away with a laundry list of problems, including bills, family disputes, and expectations that family interactions and intimacy will spring back to pre-war levels . . . It may take some service members and family members time to readjust . . ."[75] It is difficult for a family to adjust to the fact that even if their reservist has not suffered a major injury, they are not welcoming home the same reservist as the one they saw deployed. Their reservist has been changed profoundly by the Iraq War, but often the emotional, relational, and spiritual impact is not at all visible. The reservist's family has changed as well. Therefore, both parties have to readjust to one another.

Arguably the most significant and challenging aspect of reintegration has to do with the reunion of couples, as they are faced with a variety of relational challenges. The gift of honeymoon is obvious, but reintegration is more complex. Lapp et al. describe post-deployment as a period of readjustment for couples as they searched for a *new normal*.[76] The *new normal* consists of the acknowledgement that both individuals have changed as a result of the deployment through time, circumstances, and/or necessity. Reintegration into relational intimacy depends to a large extent on whether couples can deal with the reality that they both have changed during the deployment. The *new normal* for a reservist's spouse holds the challenge of readjusting from the deployment, when the spouse's circumstances included changes in household chores, social/relational interactions, and/or parenting.

Another relational and/or emotional challenge occurs when a reservist's family experiences their reservist returning physically wounded or disabled. In some cases, the injuries require an adjustment in their expressions of love and intimacy—for example, when spouses and children have

75. Molitor, Palomares, and Sammons, "Resilience in a Time of War."
76. Lapp et al., "Stress and Coping," 45–46.

to adjust to not being able to hold hands with a reservist whose hands have been lost. Reservists' families typically try not to display their emotional reactions; they attempt to be supportive of their reservist, but this is challenging for most families.

Families are also at some risk when their reservist has contracted a communicable and unfamiliar disease, such as leishmaniasis, which I discussed earlier. Reservists can reasonably expect to return to their civilian homes from a deployment in the Iraq War, while unknowingly infected with the disease, without showing any symptoms of leishmaniasis for a few years after their deployment.[77]

An immediate challenge to reintegration is that, unless they are seriously injured, reservists may face another deployment. How can reservists fully reintegrate into their civilian world when they are constantly under the threat that any day they might have to return to the hardship and horrors of combat? It is not easy to navigate one world or culture, but it is even more difficult to navigate two. Musheno and Ross describe Travis, a reservist trying to reintegrate. "With civilian life interrupted for three deployments over the span of two years, Travis struggled to keep his relationship with his girlfriend intact . . . Travis now bitterly distrusts the military organization that he views as causing such great interruptions to his civilian life . . . When we spoke with him in the spring of 2004, he was back in college for the third time and living in constant fear and uncertainty that the military, stretched thin in Iraq and Afghanistan, could call him and the company to active duty again."[78]

Travis is one example of numerous reservists whose relationships and goals were disrupted or derailed by the Iraq War. I was, in 2010, serving on a chapel team in Southern California that consisted of six chaplains and two chaplain assistants. The unpredictability and disparity of deployments is exemplified by the experience of this chapel team. In my almost six years with this reserve chapel team, one chaplain was deployed to both Afghanistan and Kuwait for six months each time; one chaplain was deployed to Qatar for three months; one chaplain assistant was deployed to Afghanistan for six months; two chaplains and one chaplain assistant were preparing for deployment to South Korea for a few weeks; and one chaplain was preparing to be deployed to Djibouti for six months. Every chaplain and chaplain assistant on my chapel team who was deployed and/or was preparing to be

77. U.S. Under Secretary for Health, "Guidance," 3.

78. Musheno and Ross, *Deployed*, 13.

deployed had a full-time civilian job, families they cared about deeply, and families who cared for them as well.

Admiral Michael Mullen, former Chairman of the Joint Chiefs of Staff, is concerned about reintegration of mobilized military personnel who "returned home on Friday and were back to work on Monday . . . It's too fast and too much."[79] It is not the case that reservists do not want to return home, but they find it extremely difficult to relate to home, especially after serving in combat. "Paul, a 38-year-old reservist from Charleston, South Carolina, believes that he is a different person since going to Iraq. Before deployment, he saw himself as carefree and sociable. Now, disillusioned by war, he can't trust people . . . His wife describes him as cold and bitter toward people and the world—yes, even toward their dog."[80]

Active duty personnel return to active duty bases built to specialize in war, so these bases are much better prepared than are civilian communities both to send soldiers to war and to receive soldiers returning from war. Injured active duty personnel return to a base with medical facilities equipped to support their long-term recovery and rehabilitation. Active duty soldiers have more opportunities to talk with other soldiers who have also served in combat or in the same area of the world. Post-deployment (and pre-deployment) conversations with other soldiers who have gone through deployment are an invaluable part of reintegration, as the stories offer unofficial, but valuable, details and processing of experiences that help to build confidence and rebuild a sense of assured familiarity. Active duty bases usually have professionals ready to assist returning soldiers with emotional, spiritual, or relational needs—a chaplain, a marriage and family therapist, a psychiatrist—all of whom may have personal experiences of combat or, at the very least, have been trained to deal with soldiers in combat-related situations.

However, in contrast to active duty personnel, a returned reservist may be the only one, or one of few persons, from their employer, neighborhood, and/or faith community who has been through deployment and combat. Consequently, reservists will often not have the opportunity to routinely engage anyone in their civilian community who has experienced the Iraq War or any other combat situation. Reservists are in an especially complicated situation when they experience any difficulties in reintegration

---

79. "Joint Chiefs of Staff Chairman: TRICARE Tops Guards, Reserve Families' Concerns."

80. Armstrong, Best, and Domenici, *Courage after Fire*, 127.

because, unlike their active duty contemporaries, they eventually have to return to a non-military environment. Reservists' complex circumstances are shown in the following example: they are often challenged "by their combat experience and struggle to fit back into civilian lives in which employers, coworkers, and friends demonstrate limited understanding of or patience with their readjustment difficulties."[81]

The reservists have been deeply affected; they need resources, people, and organizations willing to understand and help support their return to civilian culture. It can be extremely disappointing for reservists to encounter people who do not understand, or who underestimate, their sacrificial service in the Iraq War or other military conflicts. They are forced to try their best to not lose hope in what may appear to be a hopeless situation.

Reservists who have injuries often return from the Iraq War to discover civilian medical resources ill-equipped to help manage the range of combat-related wounds they bring home. The unavailability or insufficiency of needed services causes further alienation between the reservists and their military and civilian communities. Time and again the trauma of battle causes reservists to return home with psychiatric problems. One common condition is post-traumatic stress disorder (PTSD), a diagnosis that is increasingly common in our military reserves, specifically since the Iraq War. Various forms of PTSD are causing the reserves to rely on mental health professionals to help the reservists remain fit for duty in the Iraq War. PTSD can manifest itself in different ways and can be triggered by situations at home that remind the reservist of dangerous situations in which they were wounded. For instance: "Damita, an Army reservist from New York City, noticed that since returning from Iraq, when she is out walking and sees people dressed with turbans or hears Arabic being spoken, she begins sweating and becomes panicky."[82] I have counseled many reservists who struggle with functioning in the civilian world, because of their Iraq War deployment. Intuitively, we understand that there are major differences between the United States and Iraq. However, those differences may become difficult for soldiers to identify when their minds have not left their combat experiences in the past or fully processed those experiences in order to move forward in their civilian environment.

A psychological challenge facing many reservists during reintegration is a condition called adjustment disorder, in which simple everyday tasks are

81. "No Thanks for Your Service," 36.

82. Armstrong, Best, and Domenici, *Courage after Fire*, 16.

difficult because, for the reservist, they are closely associated in some way with their combat experience. For example, upon his return from the Iraq War, one reservist grapples with adjusting to driving: "Toby is a Guardsman who has just returned home to Sandusky, Ohio, from an eighteen-month tour in Iraq, after being extended twice. He served in the transportation unit there and went on multiple convoys, constantly under threat of fire and bombings. Since returning home, Toby has had a hard time driving, especially on streets where there are many cars and pedestrians. He now avoids main thoroughfares, run errands on off-hours, and drives much faster than is safe so he can get to his destination as quickly as possible."[83]

Another common manifestation of adjustment disorder happens when the reservists return from Iraq but are preoccupied with concern for those with whom they served. For example, one reservist's sleep is disturbed by scenes from his deployment: "Jacob, an Army Reserve medic from St. Louis, Missouri, can't stop wondering if the men and women he triaged lived, or died. At night as he tries to sleep, images of the injured service men and women he tried to save flood his mind."[84] Family and friends may experience difficulty welcoming home their loved one who is now a physically or psychiatrically disabled Iraq War veteran. Reservists who experience serious physical or psychiatric injuries may not be able to resume their civilian employment, or may even lose their employment because of protracted recovery. Even if they do return to their civilian jobs, their employers are now working with an employee quite different from the one they hired and anticipated to return. Coworkers may struggle to adjust to disabled Iraq War veterans returning to their prior employment.

All these losses increase the isolation and despair felt by many returning reservists. It is not surprising, then, that an increasing number of reservists who have served in Iraq choose to commit suicide. I have counseled several reservists who struggle with suicidal ideation. I have also worked on suicide prevention and suicide intervention teams with reservists and have participated along with a mental health professional officer on a panel discussing suicide. Too many reservists commit suicide: "Suicides among Army and Air National Guard and Reserve troops have spiked this year, and the military is at a loss to explain why. Sixty-five members of the Guard and Reserve took their own lives during the first six months of 2010, compared with forty-two for the same period in 2009. The grim tally is

83. Ibid., 13.
84. Ibid., 113.

further evidence that suicides continue to plague the military even though it's stepped up prevention efforts through counseling and mental health awareness programs."[85] Many reservists admit that the current expectations placed upon them in relation to the Iraq War are too much. Jeremy Easton, a sergeant with eight years of active duty and six years as a reservist, explains: "One year was rough [in Iraq]. We did it, so I guess a year is feasible. But you've got guys goin' out now that are looking at eighteen months and twenty-four months. That's too much. That's too much to ask somebody who's got a whole other life to take care of."[86]

The reservists' anxiety arises from their complex tasks and their feeling that they are unable to find a healthy balance between their military community and their civilian community. Navy Admiral Mike Mullen, former Chairman of the Joint Chiefs of Staff, during a recent talk about the suicide problem with troops in South Korea, suggested some of the precipitants of suicidality: "It is the separation from our families, it is the lack of a support structure in our personal lives sometimes, financial challenges, relationships."[87] Admiral Mullen correctly brings to light some of the contributing factors that cause reservists to commit suicide. Unfortunately, we are realizing more often that the trauma of war follows soldiers home. Here is one case in point: "Since returning home to Valparaiso, Indiana, from Iraq, Andria, a Marine reservist, can't sleep. She dreams about a suicide bomber who detonated 20 yards from her and several other Marines."[88] This reservist had difficulty sleeping, and had unpleasant dreams when she did sleep. Reservists, like everyone else, need adequate sleep to function in an optimal manner in dealing with their families and their civilian employment.

Suicide can also result from emotional and physical problems that have gone undetected for a substantial period of time—often the person in distress, their loved ones, and even their physicians miss the warning signs. Identifying the contributing factors is an important component in reducing suicide, and in the next section I will discuss strategies to eliminate some of some of these contributing factors. I have participated in both suicide prevention and suicide intervention, and I have found that the reservists having the most difficulty are the ones who have been deployed to Iraq

---

85. Goldstein. "Suicides Increase a Mystery, Guard and Reserve," C2.

86. Musheno and Ross, *Deployed*, 6.

87. Goldstein. "Suicides Increase a Mystery," C2.

88. Armstrong, Best, and Domenici, *Courage after Fire*, 13.

or another combat location. Returning home from the Iraq War may be an answered prayer for some reservists, but many religious and spiritual issues remain unresolved for others who are spiritually challenged when they return from their deployment. "Common beliefs that veterans returning from Iraq or Afghanistan have about spirituality and faith include: I no longer have faith that God exists. My higher power betrayed me. I'm too bad to be loved by a higher power. How could there be a God, given what I've seen? God can't protect anybody. God isn't fair."[89] The quote suggests several religious and spiritual issues: disruption of reservists' view of and relationship with God, the risk of death, and moral questions related to what they have witnessed and/or to their own actions in combat. Those particular spiritual issues do not always lead to suicide, but they can.

Spiritual Life during Post-Deployment

After returning home, reservists usually have a host of spiritual questions, but very few answers. More important than answers, reservists tend not to have as many people in their lives who are familiar with the military or interested in military life, as compared to their active duty colleagues. Reservists typically have fewer people with whom to have extensive discussions about their circumstances related to the Iraq War. All the same factors are present that existed with pre-deployment and deployment, but there are others related to post-deployment: feeling angry at God, because of their emotional, physical, psychiatric, relational, and/or spiritual wound(s); feeling spiritually isolated and disconnected from their faith community; and losing their faith and/or hope for the future. It is a major problem when reservists cannot find anyone who is willing to have thoughtful conversations about the intersection of spirituality and the reservists' experience during the war.

The anger felt by reservists and their families can manifest itself in their desire to give up on life because of their negative experience of unanswered prayers and disappointment resulting from their deployment. This anger can also translate into spiritual pessimism and/or a condemnation of God. Their spiritual isolation can manifest itself in a reluctance to attend worship services, a refusal to participate in religious activities, and/or a decision to discontinue their relationship with God.

89. Ibid., 138–39.

It has been noted that some soldiers engage in criminal behavior during deployment. Loss of faith and hope can also contribute to a soldier's involvement in post-deployment criminal behavior. Soldiers can lose their faith and hope from their harsh experiences in Iraq and/or from their inability to readjust to their post-deployment environment. Steve Lopez, a reporter for the *Los Angeles Times*, wrote about the struggle of one soldier who fell into a life of crime and drug addiction after his return from the Iraq War.[90] An unfortunate reality is that some reservists' wounded souls may turn them toward a life of crime.

In this chapter, we have examined a range of physical, emotional, relational, psychiatric, and spiritual challenges of both reservists and their families, related to reservists' Iraq War service during pre-deployment, deployment, and post-deployment. The reservists' families do not take a military oath to protect and defend our national interests, but they endure many of the unanticipated dangers, uncertain threats, and possibilities of peril experienced by their reservists.

In the next chapter I will discuss the ways in which pastors and chaplains, through a soul care approach, can help lead efforts to offer care to reservists and their families.

90. Lopez, "Combat Veteran's Struggle of the Soul," A2.

Chapter 5

Recommendations for
a Soul Care Approach

T HIS FINAL CHAPTER HAS three main sections. The first section addresses expectations chaplains and pastors should bring to soul care with reservists and their families. The second section offers strategies of soul care following the structure of Pavlicin's framework and by discussing crisis counseling. The final section identifies directions for fruitful research on this topic in the future.[1]

It is very important to note that, although chaplains and pastors are addressed repeatedly throughout this research, lay persons in military chapels and in civilian churches also have a responsibility for caring for others.[2] They should be led by their chaplains and pastors in providing soul care. Furthermore, it may be that others will be able to apply these recommendations to reservists and their families who live in their neighborhoods. Such families are especially in need of soul care, which may help them as they coexist in the civilian and military worlds.

1. Pavlicin, *Surviving Deployment*, 6.
2. Stone, *Caring Church*, 3.

CHAPLAINS' AND PASTORS' EXPECTATIONS

Theological and Pastoral Transformations

Challenges have a way of changing us, whether we experience the challenge or witness the struggle of others. Challenges, especially tragedies, can bend, break, and even eliminate certain ways of thinking of oneself, others, and the world. This is true of my experience as an Air Force chaplain reservist. Many of my experiences have been exciting, educational, and informative as they relate to military life. On the other hand, some of my chaplain experiences of providing soul care to reservists and their families negatively impacted by the Iraq War have convinced me that unfortunate events of life will not always be easily explained within traditional denominational or religious paradigms. Years ago, I realized that agreement in theologies or religious affiliations is not necessary in order to care for someone effectively. My theological/pastoral transformation has matured, in that I ask more questions and give fewer statements. My pastoral care and counseling experience has required me to listen more and allow the military community to grieve, regardless of whether this includes anger, disappointment, and/or unfamiliar ways of interpreting life. I have listened to reservists and their families share with me some of the most unorthodox and unusual interpretations of their challenges. Tragedies can create various responses. What is necessary on the part of soul care providers is the allowance of the Holy Spirit to transmit grace, love, forgiveness, and redemption for reservists and their families. I have learned that God often works in ways that are unknown and unexpected. I encourage all people who desire to provide soul care to not allow your embedded theologies and religious beliefs to hinder the possible healing process for reservists and their families.

Pastors Not in the Military

Civilian pastors should expect to have the possibility to care for a higher number of reservists and their families than military chaplains. One main reason for this is that these families rarely, and may not ever, visit a military facility or attend military events. Civilian pastors live in closer proximity to reservists and their families than military chaplains. Simply put, there are more civilian pastors to offer a soul care approach than there are military chaplains, who may not be able to connect with all reservists and their families for several reasons that include geographical distance and time constraints. Therefore, civilian pastors' presence and efforts are appreciated and needed in order to reach reservists and their families who are negatively impacted by the Iraq War and who live all across the United States.

Reasonable Outcomes to a Soul Care Approach

It is important for chaplains and pastors to understand that a soul care approach should not be expected to easily solve all the problems affecting reservists and their families because of service in the Iraq War. Chaplains and pastors should remember their purpose is not to cure, but it is to care. Soul care does not seek to eliminate challenges by making them disappear. Soul care thoughtfully examines challenges through lenses of hope, understanding, forgiveness, and redemption. Soul care seeks to empower reservists and their families to not adopt an attitude of defeatism or despair. It is essential to outline realistic expectations for soul care providers and receivers in order to help prevent confusion and disappointment. Soul care providers should communicate reasonable outcomes to reservists and their families. Such outcomes can include identifying and obtaining useful resources, contacting mental health professionals, increasing the ability to forgive and to receive forgiveness, and seeking spiritual renewal through religious practices.

Reservists' and their families' worlds can crash in any of the eight stages within pre-deployment, deployment, and post-deployment. The crash can consist of familiar spiritual and theological framework(s) breaking into pieces to the point of being inoperative. Soul care calls for chaplains and pastors to be sufficiently patient to examine these broken pieces, with the intent to help bring wholeness. Many reservists and their families will be unable to easily or neatly put their broken pieces together again into their pre-war ideology. Their combat and post-war experiences may have taken them beyond any standard orthodoxy within traditional religious paradigms. Soul care will require chaplains and pastors to be open to multiple faith traditions that are reflected in a religiously diverse military. Chaplains and pastors may have to be receptive to new spiritual or theological interpretations in order to assist in the healing process within war-related situations. Furthermore, they should be willing to go beyond their own theological comfort zones in order to help reservists and their families experience God's activity in meaningful ways. Soul care seeks to help bring healing, liberation, and relief to reservists and their families with wounds from the Iraq War. As a chaplain reservist, I have often had to go beyond my spiritual and theological comfort zones in providing pastoral care and counseling, in order to help soldiers deal with the broken pieces of their lives. I now encourage more chaplains, pastors, and people of faith to do the same in the specific manner of pastoral care and counseling referred to as soul care.

Reservists' and their families' souls are suffering from the Iraq War's various negative effects on their lives, as I explored and described earlier. I have noted that, although the Iraq War has officially ended, the United States continues to send soldiers to that region, and they continue to get wounded or killed. Pastoral support in the form of soul care is needed throughout each of the three stages of pre-deployment, deployment, and post-deployment. Pavlicin recommends in general talking to a military chaplain or civilian, and she highlights the clergy's obligation to maintain confidentiality.[3] In order to connect with and understand reservists and their families, it will be useful for military chaplains as well as civilian clergy to be familiar with and sensitive to the three phases and eight stages we have explored, using Pavlicin's framework.[4] Having used this framework to explore the difficulties experienced by reservists and their families affected by the Iraq War, we will use it one final time to articulate a soul care approach to guide chaplains and pastors as they seek to console, support, and help reservists and their families to find healing.

PHASE I: PRE-DEPLOYMENT AND PREPARATION

Regardless of the duration of pre-deployment and preparation, chaplains and pastors can offer meaningful care to support reservists and their families during this important first phase, in which soul care during pre-deployment has the ability to positively influence deployment and post-deployment.

Stage 1: Shock/Denial/Anger

As an Air Force chaplain reservist, I have been contacted by reservists and/or their families on many occasions shortly after they were notified about

3. Pavlicin, *Surviving Deployment*, 228.
4. Ibid., 6.

their scheduled deployment to the Iraq War. For reservists themselves, this first stage generally does not last very long. They know the importance of redirecting their energy and time, away from resistance and toward actions that will benefit their families and civilian professions during the period they are to be deployed. However, the reservists' *families* tend to remain in Stage 1 a little longer. Whether with reservists or families, I have learned by experience that it is best primarily to listen to the feelings of shock, denial and anger during this stage. Though the pastor or chaplain may ask an occasional question for clarity or offer assurance of support, it will not be effective to suggest that the reservists and family strive for different emotions. Rather, it is a time to listen closely and intentionally, because they could be sharing valuable information from their soul. Soul care gives room for expression(s), even if it is shock, denial, and anger. The best statements that chaplains and pastors can offer at this stage are those that inform reservists and their families that they are valued and are allowed to feel free to reach out for support anytime as needed.

It is also appropriate for the chaplain or pastor to offer resources such as the following:

- "Family Member Pre-deployment Checklist" from the American Bar Association; "Pre-deployment Checklist" from the National Guard Family Program.[5]

- A prayer, a prayerful statement, and/or a devotional book. (It is important for the chaplain or pastor to keep in mind that this approach to soul care accepts the idea that regardless of the expressed content— even emotional, physical, economic, or political—most distress is in some major way a spiritual crisis.)[6]

- Asking the reservists and their families about the kind(s) of task(s) for which they need assistance, related to any items on the pre-deployment checklist. (It is always good for the chaplain or pastor to ask, at every phase and stage, about the issues that are causing the most frustration.)

Reservists and their families may manifest their shock, denial, and anger in a variety of ways. Soul care allows and encourages reservists and their families to express shock, denial, and anger without the pastor

---

5. American Bar Association, "Family Member Pre-deployment Checklist"; National Guard Family Program, "Family Readiness: Step 4, Pre-deployment."

6. McBride, *Spiritual Crisis*, xii.

or chaplain displaying any disapproval. Chaplains and pastors should be aware that some reservists' families have decided to join organizations that enable them to voice their anger publicly: "Military Families Speak Out is an organization of people opposed to the wars in Iraq and Afghanistan who have relatives or loved ones currently in the military . . . we know that it is our loved ones who are, or have been, or will be on the battlefront. It is our loved ones who are at risk, who have been injured or who have died as a result of these wars."[7] Military Families Speak Out claims a membership of close to four thousand families, with local chapters nationwide.[8] A similar organization, Iraq War Veterans Against the War, claims to have local chapters nationwide in addition to international chapters.[9] Within these organizations, the reservists and their families may find comfort in their anger and realize they are not alone in their anger. With those reservists and families who are angry, chaplains and pastors can seek to offer soul care by informing them of credible organizations that may help them voice their opposition to military operations in Iraq or elsewhere.

Stage 2: Anticipation of Loss

In this stage, the reservists and their families have generally calmed down and are trying to come to terms with the knowledge that deployment signals a variety of losses. Chaplains and pastors should acknowledge and affirm the various losses the reservists and their families perceive as important. I have had many reservists and their families share with me that their anticipation of loss centered on special family dates, such as a wedding anniversary or a child's birthday, as well as losing time they could be engaged in their civilian profession or education.

Reservists and their families are typically more open to public forms of soul care such as the following, which are offered as suggestions to guide both chaplains and pastors:

- Have the congregation pray for reservists and their families as part of a worship service or in a smaller setting before or after a worship service.

---

7. Military Families Speak Out, http://www.mfso.org.
8. Ibid.
9. Iraq Veterans Against the War, http://www.ivaw.org.

- Offer a day and time to meet with the reservists and their families to give them an opportunity to discuss any concerns they may have in relation to their deployment to Iraq or elsewhere. Lift up the significance of military service to the faith community with special emphasis on the sacrifices made in association with the Iraq War and other places of reservist service. This can be accomplished through various communications such as sermons, special services, prayer vigils, verbal announcements, newsletters, and websites.

- Ask the reservists and their families what fear(s) or concern(s) they are experiencing and for which they would like the chaplain or pastor to give assistance.

Soul care allows the reservists and their families to communicate for themselves exactly what they are anticipating to lose on account of the upcoming deployment. Soul care does not dictate to reservists and their families what they should or should not be concerned about losing, but the chaplain or pastor should acknowledge the significance of the person(s), place(s), and/or thing(s) the reservists and their families anticipate losing.

Stage 3: Emotional Detachment

This can be the most complex stage in Phase I. I have seen reservists and their families, as they continue their preparation for deployment, become emotionally detached from one another and from other people—each family member in his or her own way. When this happens, more concrete preparations, such as the "Family Member Pre-deployment Checklist" from the American Bar Association, become less important to them and more difficult for them to complete. And yet it has also been my experience that this emotional detachment does not prevent significant conversations, which can take place just before the actual deployment. For example, I have had several discussions about the possibility of death with reservists anticipating deployment. I have found that in these conversations the soldiers' focal point is not the possibility of their death or preoccupation with their death, because it does not help them achieve their mission. Rather, when reservists lift up the topic of death to me in private conversation, they have usually not been afraid to die; they are usually more concerned about their family's well-being in the event of their death. The reservists usually talk about how their family members might react in the event of their death. I listen and give them plenty of room to talk.

I know the topic of the possibility of death is usually a difficult one for any person to discuss under most circumstances. It is important for chaplains and pastors to allow the reservists to share any and all concerns they may be experiencing about death. For example, one reservist shared with me a concern for her pet in the event of her death. At that particular moment, the reservist's pet was of primary concern and it was essential for me to convey that this was an important matter, not trivial. Soul care requires the caregiver to respect everything the reservists hold as important in their lives and in their possible death. This stage will probably require soul care to be applied briefly, because of the emotional detachment dynamic. As I will discuss more fully in a later section of this chapter, chaplains and pastors should remember that brief counseling sessions can be just as effective as, or better than, longer counseling sessions and multiple encounters.[10]

PHASE II: DEPLOYMENT/SEPARATION

In this phase, I will be addressing the care given by deployed military chaplains offering soul care to deployed reservists, as well as non-deployed chaplains and pastors dealing with the families. During the military operations in the Berlin airlift in 1948, a general took the time to admonish his colleagues that attention must be fairly divided between the soldier and the family at home. "General Hoyt S. Vandenberg . . . sent a message to all commanding generals in which he said: I am deeply concerned about the welfare of dependents left behind . . . We must do our utmost to provide the assistance which normally would be the concern of the family heads who were moved so suddenly . . . I desire a report each month on action taken and results obtained . . . [and] urge chaplains to visit the families of all Airlift personnel and render needed assistance. [United States Air Forces in Europe] Staff Chaplain Marteney reported an improvement in morale when chaplains got on the job."[11] Chaplains and pastors who minister stateside and in deployed settings are of equal value to reservists and their families. What happens to them during deployment will have repercussions in post-deployment; therefore, it is important for families to be in the same shape or even better shape to receive their reservists when they return home.

10. Stone, *Brief Pastoral Counseling*, 7.

11. Jorgensen, *Air Force Chaplains*, 211–12.

Stage 4: Disorientation/Depression

Those clergy who minister to families stateside should be mindful that reservists' families may find it difficult to function normally in their reservists' absence. Chaplains and pastors may offer soul care to these families during deployment in various ways, including the following:

- Have the congregation pray for the reservists as part of a worship service or in a smaller setting before or after a worship service in the presence of the reservists' families, but their attendance is not required.

- Offer a day/time to meet with the reservists' families to give them an opportunity to discuss any concerns they may have in relation to their reservists' deployment. It is important for the chaplain or pastor to be able to utilize the referral process when appropriate.

- Lift up the significance of military service to the faith community—with special emphasis on the sacrifices made in association with the Iraq War and other forms of service—through various communications such as sermons, verbal announcements, newsletters, and websites.

- Have the congregation mail the reservists cards, letters, and/or care packages that will be useful. I typically do not recommend that civilians (outside of the reservists' families) email soldiers deployed to war, because of the soldiers' time constraints, among other reasons. Additionally, it is important that all communication sent to deployed soldiers be *good news*. Chaplains who are ministering in deployed settings should be mindful that soldiers may find it difficult to function at their best during this stage. Chaplains should offer soul care to soldiers in various ways that can include the following:

  - Have the chapel team pray for the soldiers as part of a worship service or in a smaller setting before or after a worship service in the presence of the soldiers, but their attendance is not required.

  - Offer a day/time to meet with the soldiers to give them an opportunity to discuss any concerns they may have in relation to the Iraq War or other deployment. It is important for the chaplain or pastor to be able to utilize the referral process when appropriate.

  - Lift up the significance of military service to the faith community, with special emphasis on the sacrifices made in association with the Iraq War and other forms of service. This can be done through such communications as sermons, verbal announcements, newsletters, and websites. Have the chapel team mail the reservists cards, letters and/or care packages that will be useful.

- Soul care does not perceive the disorientation/depression stage as passing and/or a stage to be taken lightly. Soul care recognizes the devastation that can occur to soldiers during this stage, and seeks to acknowledge and help alleviate the particular condition(s).

Stage 5: Adaptation

At this stage, soldiers usually more fully accept the responsibilities of their military deployment. Chaplains ministering in deployed settings should be mindful that even when soldiers adapt to their deployed environment(s), challenges remain. Chaplain Michael Dugal claims that "the reality of war eats away at the Soldier's spirit. War creates a religious and spiritual vacuum in the Soldier."[12] From this point of view, for most reservists, soul care is a crucial element in their mission. "The more dangerous the mission, the more vital chaplains are to its success. The nearly fourteen hundred chaplains in the U.S. armed forces—all Christian but for about thirty Jewish and fifteen Muslim clergy—must be on-the-spot counselors to men and women living through a kind of trauma that few civilians will ever experience. They prepare soldiers to kill and to die without losing their souls."[13]

Soul care understands that soldiers' adaptability does not equate to their being comfortable in deployed settings. Soul care can help reduce soldiers' fears, by helping to normalize those fears and providing environments where it is safe to talk about them rather than obsessing or worrying about them. Chaplains should be able to discuss the possibility of death openly with their soldiers. Discussions about death should be focused on honorable deaths related to protecting and defending one's country. However, emphasizing in discussions the importance of living life to the fullest in an honorable manner, even in war, should always be primary in deployed settings.

12. Dugal, "Affirming the Soldier's Spirit," 16.
13. Dreher, "Ministers of War."

Chaplains and pastors ministering stateside should be sensitive to the reservists' families' adjustment(s) to their new realities. If children are involved, it is important that they be given adequate attention. Too often, reservists' children are overlooked while the adults are given most of the attention. Children have souls, too, and how they are cared for or not cared for will be influential in their human development. Reservists' children are suffering. "Military children also warrant particular attention. First, children of reservists face the challenge of some of the demands of military family life such as separation and concerns about the military parent being injured or killed, and yet these families are not integrated into the military culture."[14] It would be good to create events and/or sponsor various programs that are primarily for reservists' children. In my experience working at civilian churches for over a decade, most congregations would agree that when churches have relevant programs for the children, it will usually bring in the entire family. Chaplains and pastors should become familiar with the following groups, which offer help with caring for reservists' children:

- Military Child Education Coalition[15]
- Serving Suddenly Military Children[16]
- Military Home Front: Supporting Our Troops & Their Families[17]

Children are typically among the most vulnerable segments in any society and the children of the military are not an exception. The chaplain or pastor should ask a series of questions to the reservists' entire family, with special attention to the children, about the media's influence on them. A primary recommendation to the parent(s) includes highlighting the importance of filtering and interpreting the media. One pastoral recommendation to the parent(s) includes encouraging their children to watch only certain television programs, listen to certain radio stations, and explore certain websites. The soul care plan of action will look different for children of various ages. Furthermore, it is beneficial to have discussions with children about their perception or experience(s) with the media coverage of the Iraq War or other conflicts in which their parent(s) may be involved.

14. Ender, "Voices from the Backseat," 157.

15. See information at http://www.militarychild.org.

16. Access information at http://www.nasbhc.org.

17. See the Web site at http://www.militaryhomefront.dod.mil.

Stage 6: Anticipation of Homecoming

The reservists and their families look forward to seeing one another again. This stage can cause a lot of anxiety, because it will have been a while since the reservists and their families have spent time together. The deployed chaplain should convey to the soldiers that they have given honorable service to their country. The chaplain should also remind the soldiers that time has not stopped while they have been deployed, and their families have had to reorder themselves in numerous ways in their absence. Thompson and Wetterstrom offer some illustrative details: "Excitement about a soldier's return is often clouded with doubts. Will my dad still love me? Will my son have changed? What if my wife doesn't like how I raised the kids while she was gone? Soldiers are also conflicted about reuniting with their family. Will I fit back into my home life? Will I still have a role? Will the kids know who I am? Does my spouse still love me?"[18] These are common and important questions, and they will not be easily resolved without dedicated work. Chaplains should offer soul care in a variety of ways to help the soldiers return home with realistic expectations. For example, chaplains offering soul care would not suggest that a soldier's home has magically or miraculously changed for the better because he or she is returning from war. Soul care focuses more on the pragmatic and practical rather than the ideal.

For chaplains and pastors ministering stateside, I always recommend that the reservists' families make a schedule of a few activities their reservists enjoyed prior to deployment. At the same time I caution them against scheduling too many activities; the returning reservists do need time to rest. However, they should not be left alone in a room to sleep by themselves all week; it is a delicate balance. Keep in mind that the reservists are returning from war, so they should not return home to a laundry list of troubles or the popularly named "honey do" list. The chaplain or pastor should remind the families that their reservists will most likely be a combination of tired, restless, excited, and depressed, and perhaps also devastated by their deployment experience.

18. Thompson and Wetterstrom. *Beyond the Yellow Ribbon*, 47.

PHASE III:
POST-DEPLOYMENT/HOMECOMING/REUNION

Stage 7: Honeymoon

As previously noted, this is one of the shortest stages in the entire cycle. This stage, which typically includes handshakes, hugs, kisses, and celebrations, can last for a few minutes or extend to a few months. If the chaplain or pastor is present, it is appropriate for him or her to give a pastoral prayer of thanksgiving. Additionally, the following events and resources are recommended for chaplains and pastors during this stage:

- Host a party or a gathering at a church, community center, or some other convenient place to celebrate the reservist's return.

- Offer to do a special bible study, devotional, or prayer service in the reservist's home, by yourself or with a small group of leaders from the church or community. (It would be wise to get the reservist's and her or his family's approval of the list of people who may be attending this celebratory religious/spiritual gathering).

- Instead of a care package, mail a "thank you package" to the home that consists of cards, letters, and other gifts that show appreciation for the sacrifices and service offered by both the reservist and her or his family.[19]

- Become familiar with "Resilience in a Time of War: Homecoming," from the American Psychological Association,[20] and the Web site of the National Center for Post-Traumatic Stress Disorder.[21]

The reunion stage should not occur exclusively with the reservists and their families, excluding participation by the chaplain or pastor. Obviously, the reservists and their families should have some private and quiet time throughout all the stages. However, the proper involvement of a chaplain or pastor within their reach during the "honeymoon" stage gives them a sense of consolation as well as a person to contact quickly in case of an unexpected emergency.

19. Ibid.
20. Molitor, Palomares, and Sammons, "Resilience in a Time of War."
21. National Center for Post-Traumatic Stress Disorder, http://www.ptsd.va.gov.

Stage 8: Reintegration

This last stage is usually the longest stage in the entire cycle. Too many veterans of war are broken in body or spirit by their wartime experiences and they struggle for years trying to put their lives back together.[22] During the reintegration period, reservists and their families struggle to readjust to one another and all their new circumstances.

The reservists must adjust to a new environment in which their safety is not constantly threatened by IEDs and other combat concerns. The reservists must reintegrate into living in their civilian home rather than military quarters, their civilian family rather than other soldiers, their civilian clothes rather than a military uniform, among many other issues. This takes time. Chaplains and pastors should remind the reservists that adjusting to civilian life can be a slow process.

The reservists' families must adjust to having their reservist return to their home, facing a redistribution of chores and experiencing in an up close and personal manner the aftereffects of the Iraq War on their reservist. This, too, takes time. Chaplains and pastors should remind the reservists' families that adjusting to their reservist can be a slow process.

Reservists and their families are often an afterthought, or not thought of at all, by some faith communities. Reservists and their families can benefit from a community willing to help them process their pre-deployment, deployment, and post-deployment experiences. Some of their processing should take place individually, and some collectively. Marty Mendenhall suggests one contribution of the chaplain [and pastor] during reintegration for the reservists: "A chaplain [and pastor] may be a vital resource in assisting soldiers in reframing their war experience, and may also strengthen a soldier's ability to cope following a combat episode by lending psychological and spiritual support. A chaplain [and pastor] may serve as a model of acceptance, compassion, and forgiveness."[23]

This approach to soul care does not advocate a certain image of family roles or other intrapersonal or interpersonal dynamics; instead, it does advocate grace, patience, and forgiveness to be offered by the chaplain or pastor and to be exercised by all parties involved.

22. Thompson and Wetterstrom. *Beyond the Yellow Ribbon*, vii.
23. Mendenhall, "Chaplains in Mental Health," 4.

Chaplains and pastors should help soldiers reintegrate into the lives of their families.[24] It is recommended that they offer very practical forms of support for the reservists' reintegration, such as newspaper articles or conversations to inform them about significant events that occurred in their civilian world during their deployment. Bad news should always be kept to a minimum and should not be one of the first messages conveyed to the reservists. Soul care's aim is to help alleviate and heal the devastation and shock to reservists and their families caused by the Iraq War and other deployments.

Crisis Counseling

Soul care is for people of all ages, races, nationalities, genders, and faith traditions. This recommended soul care approach is not only pragmatic, but also systematic in application. Chaplains and pastors should be prepared to offer soul care to reservists and their families by means of Clinebell's ABCD method of crisis counseling during pre-deployment, deployment, and post-deployment. "The ABCD method employs the principles of crisis counseling to help yourself and/or others cope constructively with many types of crises: Achieve a trusting helper-helpee relationship with [the reservist/ reservists' families], Boil down the problem to its smaller or major parts with [the reservist/reservists' families], Challenge the [reservist/reservists' families] to take constructive action on some part of the problem, Develop an ongoing growth-action plan with [the reservist/ reservists' families]."[25] One significant aspect of the ABCD method is that it includes a systematic approach to address the problems that are of immediate concern to the reservists and their families, rather than becoming distracted by minor challenges that can wait to receive attention in the near future. Another significant aspect of the ABCD method is its inclusive, holistic approach, which can address emotional, physical, psychiatric, relational, and spiritual challenges of the reservists and their families impacted by the Iraq War.

24. Dreher, "Ministers of War."

25. Clinebell, *Basic Types of Pastoral Care and Counseling*, 205–8. Howard Clinebell uses the ABCD method in a number of his books. In *Well Being* (222), he references psychiatrist Warren A. Jones, who wrote the essay "The A-B-C Method of Crisis Management." Clinebell also mentions that he added the "D" to the method. Howard Stone, in his book *The Caring Church* (37), also acknowledges Jones' creation of the ABC method of crisis and that many people revised it for their purposes of care.

All four components of the ABCD method are essential. Let us begin by explaining the importance of each of the four. The first step is to *achieve* a trusting helper-helpee relationship. This first step is paramount, because it gives the reservists and their families the opportunity to be open and honest about their problems. When this first step is completed, they are able to identify a safe space to reveal and share their problems, often quite personal in nature, with the chaplain or pastor. Chaplains and pastors should identify themselves as supporters of reservists and their families, in various forms of communication to the public and especially in their local communities. This can be done through speeches, sermons, websites, posters, church ministry committees, workshops, and newspaper advertisements, among other options for extending hospitable messages. It is important for reservists and their families to recognize the pastor or chaplain as an individual who is willing to provide soul care in this particular situation. Little progress, if any, can be made without chaplains and pastors establishing a trusting helper-helpee relationship with reservists and families negatively impacted by the Iraq War. Once this trusting relationship has been established, there is a specific direction for this specific care.

The second step of the ABCD method for this soul care technique is to help *boil down* the problem into actionable parts with the reservists and their families. This step enables the chaplain or pastor to identify problems that can or should be addressed immediately. It requires the chaplain or pastor intentionally to do more listening than talking, because the reservists and their families are usually intimately aware of their own challenges. If words are needed from the chaplain or pastor to advance communication, they should be in the form of statements or questions attempting to further detect the problem(s) so as to be able to determine whether or not the problems are emotional, physical, psychiatric, relational, and/or spiritual. As was previously noted, it may not always be easy or possible to categorize problems with these labels, because categories often overlap. I suggest using a questionnaire in order to assist chaplains and pastors in helping reservists and their families boil down the challenge(s) into a manageable state of affairs (see Appendix A). The questionnaire will be elaborated upon at the end of this section.

The third step is to *challenge* the reservists and their families to take constructive action on some part of the problem. This step involves the chaplain or pastor offering more statements than in step two. While step two primarily consists of inquiry as to past and current problems, step three entails mostly a combination of encouragement, confrontation, and inspiration for action. The chaplain or pastor must realize that he or she cannot resolve the families' problems without the reservists and their families taking principal responsibility to invest their efforts in managing the specified problems. Question four of the questionnaire, regarding assistance, can be highlighted to help convey the importance of the reservists' and their families' actions in wanting help, meaning they also have a significant role to play. The chaplain or pastor should impress this importance upon them in a challenging, yet compassionate, manner (necessary for not allowing the specified problem to go unattended). It is crucial that the chaplain or pastor be aware of the role religion is playing in the lives of the reservist and their family members, and that they convey consistent messages about religion's potential to be of help. Aphrodite Mataskis, a licensed counseling psychologist, writes: "Some veterans have been told that they can free themselves from the emotional scars of battle if they focus on their faith rather than their feelings. Yet others have been told the opposite: that their spirituality is an escape from their feelings . . . Veterans who seek help from more than one source . . . may find that their helpers do not agree on what to put first: faith or feelings. This can lead not only to confusion but also despair."[26] Chaplains and pastors must keep in mind that reservists and their families sometimes have negative preconceived notions of faith communities, based on opinions and/or their actual experience(s). Like most methods, soul care does not provide easy solutions—no one should characterize it as having these to offer—and it should be used along with other methods of support. As the previous quote indicates, the soul care provider should not demand that the reservists and their families make a choice between faith or feelings. Faith *and* feelings are equally important to the human experience.

The fourth step is to *develop* an ongoing growth-action plan with the reservists and their families. In this step, the chaplain or pastor helps them create a plan to address the problems revealed in step two. The chaplain or pastor may take a wide variety of actions, such as making referrals, assembling resources of books and videos, and scheduling follow-up counseling sessions. The growth-action plan should be documented by the reservists and their families with some direction from the chaplain or pastor. Ideally, both would each have a copy of the ongoing growth-action plan for future reference. It is good for the chaplain to have the support of their

26. Matsakis, *Back from the Front*, 48.

chapel community and the pastor to have the support of their congregation, because this can help increase the influence and/or extend the reach of the soul care approach. For effective referral in a timely manner, it is important for chaplains and pastors to keep updated information about programs regarding traumatic brain injury, post-traumatic stress disorder, and other services that are specifically designed for veterans of the Iraq War. Several states have programs, such as Illinois' Veterans Care Program, Ohio's OHIOCares program, Rhode Island's "The Rhode Island Blueprint," Vermont's "Military, Family, and Community Network," and a similar program in the state of Washington.[27] Some nonprofit organizations have special programs for Iraq veterans, such as the U.S. Veterans Initiative, which is located in several states—Arizona, California, Hawaii, Nevada, and Texas—and Washington, DC.[28] It is important to note that there is not a specific time frame for the ABCD method to be completed from start to finish; in extremely exceptional circumstances, it can be accomplished in as little as an hour, but is more likely to take several meetings over weeks or months. Especially in regard to step four, the ongoing growth-action plan could have a limited time frame or it could go on indefinitely.

Applying the ABCD method with reservists and their families will not be easy, under the best circumstances, for several reasons: 1) it can take a substantial amount of time to accomplish step one; 2) the challenges may be difficult to hear in step two; 3) it can be wearisome to complete step three; and 4) it may be disappointing not to have follow-up opportunities or the expected results in step four. In order for pastors and chaplains to help ensure that the ABCD method is productive, a self-evaluation tool, revised from Clinebell's, may be used (see Appendix B).

It is vital for chaplains and pastors to keep good records when they offer crisis counseling to reservists and their families and to ensure that records are kept in a safe and secure place. The Appendices include documents titled "Questionnaire for Reservists and Families: Your Experience of Deployment" and "Self-Evaluation of Soul Care to Reservists and Their Families." These are tools that have been inspired by the work of Howard Clinebell.[29] I started working on these documents in 2009 while critically

27. Tanielian and Jaycox, *Invisible Wounds of War*, 401.

28. See information at the United States Veterans Initiative Web site, http://www.usvetsinc.org.

29. Clinebell, *Well Being*, 314–18.

reflecting on my work with soldiers and their families negatively impacted by the Iraq War. These documents should be stored in a secure location.

Discussion of Future Research

There is a need for additional research regarding chaplains, pastors, pastoral care and counseling, and reservists and their families. My research does not give an exhaustive account of current contributing factors related to demographics and geopolitics that could help explain communities' neglect of care for military communities. Research that focuses upon certain geographical regions, such as the East Coast, Midwest, and West Coast, is worthy of exploration. It would also be interesting to research instances during war when soldiers and/or their families experience a deepening or renewal of their spiritual life.

Another important research project would be an exclusive study on reservists' children, with the intent to empower them in order to understand and navigate successfully both the civilian and military worlds. Unfortunately, the article titled "Wartime Military Deployment and Increased Pediatric Mental and Behavioral Health Complaints" did not discuss the children of reservists.[30] Another question to research is, in what ways are towns impacted when reservists deploy? This question can be explored in an attempt to help towns prepare and set up contingency plans for when their reservists deploy. Future research should also include the examination of soldiers who are resilient during war. Those particular topics are worthy of critical exploration and research.

If our human history is only partially correct in informing us of our future state of affairs then we should be prepared for the multiple impacts of military conflict in the form of war. The quality of our human existence in the future depends on this particular research that closely examines the results when countries inevitably and violently collide with one another. Every country consists of precious individuals whose lives are valuable to be cared for even in war.

30. Gorman, Eide, and Hisle-Gorman, "Wartime Military Deployment," 2.

Appendix A

Questionnaire for Reservists and Families

Your Experience of Deployment

Date: _____

Reservist's and/or family's name: _____

Contact information: _____

This is not a test—there are no correct or incorrect answers. Before you respond to any questions, it is important to remind you that you are a valuable human being loved by God and supported by people who acknowledge the consequences of the Iraq War.

1. Are you negatively impacted by emotional, physical, psychiatric, relational, and/or spiritual problems caused by the Iraq War?

   Select One: YES   *or*   NO

2. If yes, select no more than two of the most distressing problems:

   emotional   physical   psychiatric   relational   spiritual

3. Please describe one experience with each problem, circled above, that has occurred within the past year.

_____

_____

_____

_____

4. Would you like assistance in managing the problem(s) identified above?
   Select One: YES   *or*   NO

Appendix B

Self-Evaluation of Soul Care to Reservists and Their Families[1]

Date: _____

Chaplain/Pastor and/or Congregation's name: _____

Contact information: _____

This is not a test—there are no correct or incorrect answers. Before you respond to any questions, it is important to remind you that you are a valuable human being loved by God; your noble efforts attempt to support reservists and their families impacted by the Iraq War.

Self-evaluate the soul care's effectiveness of the soul care offered by placing one of three indicators: E= Excellent; OK= Acceptable; NS= Needs Strengthening.

1. _____ The organization is designed to meet the emotional, physical, psychiatric, relational, and/or spiritual needs of reservists and their families impacted by the Iraq War.

---

1. In my development of this self-evaluation, I have drawn on Clinebell, *Well Being*, 314-18.

2. _____ The *esprit de corps* or emotional climate of the group is generally accepting and warm toward reservists and their families impacted by the Iraq War.

3. _____ The organization's goals are measurable, making it possible to know when progress has been made serving reservists and their families impacted by the Iraq War.

4. _____ There is an openness to interact and cooperate with other organizations that seek to provide support to reservists and their families impacted by the Iraq War, rather than being an exclusive or closed group.

5. _____ Members of the organization have opportunities to learn how to provide soul care to reservists and their families impacted by the Iraq War by encountering people, programs, books, and other mediums by which they can gain knowledge.

6. Please describe the action plan.

_____

_____

_____

_____

Bibliography

ARTICLES, BOOK CHAPTERS, PAMPHLETS, AND REPORTS

Alford, Deann. "Faith, Fear, War, Peace: Snapshots of the Grim and 'Happy' Ministry of Today's Military Chaplains." *Christianity Today*, December 2004, 45–48.

American Bar Association, "Family Member Pre-deployment Checklist." Online: http://apps.americanbar.org/family/military/checklist.pdf.

American Psychological Association. Presidential Task Force on Military Deployment Services for Youth, Families and Service Members. "The Psychological Needs of U.S. Military Service Members and Their Families: A Preliminary Report." Online: http://www.apa.org/about/policy/military-needs.aspx.

Army National Guard. "Legal Basis of the National Guard." Online: http://www.arng.army.mil/aboutus/history/Pages/ConstitutionalCharteroftheGuard.aspx.

Associated Press. "Death Toll Rises for Reservists." Online: http://www.military.com/NewsContent/0,13319,78441,00.html.

————. "Families Blame Vet Suicides on Lack of VA Care." Online: http://www.msnbc.msn.com/id/18908471/ns/health-mental_health/t/families-blame-vet-suicides-lack-va-care/.

Badgett, Dwight. "Preserving the Reserve Triad: Balancing Family, Civilian Job, and the Air Force." *Citizen Airmen*, April 2, 2010, 3.

Britt, Thomas W., Tiffany M. Greene-Shortridge, and Carl A. Castro. "The Stigma of Mental Health Problems in the Military." *Military Medicine* 172 (2007) 157–61.

Brown, Frank. "Ministering to an Unpopular War." *Spectrum*, Winter 2008. Online: http://www.yale.edu/divinity/notes/080522/spectrumchaplains.pdf.

Bush, George W. Executive Order 13223. "Ordering the Ready Reserve of the Armed Forces to Active Duty and Delegating Certain Authorities to the Secretary of Defense and the Secretary of Transportation." Online: http://www.presidency.ucsb.edu/ws/index.php?pid=61504.html.

Carlson, John D. "Cashing in on Religion's Currency? Ethical Challenges for a Post-Secular Military." *Review of Faith and International Affairs* 7 (2009) 51–62.

"Chaplains Muse on War Years: Lasting Bonds Formed under Combat Stress." *National Catholic Reporter*, December 15, 1995. Online: http://www.thefreelibrary

.com/Chaplains+muse+on+war+years%3a+lasting+bonds+formed+under+combat +stress.-a017917930.

Chapman, G. Clarke, Jr. "'I Recognize Religion': Terrorism and Pastoral Theology." *Quarterly Review* 24 (2004) 59–66.

Chappelle, Wayne. "An Air Force Psychologist's Collaboration with Clergy: Lessons Learned on the Battlefield of Iraq." *Journal of Psychology and Christianity* 25 (2006) 206–7.

Chartrand, Molinda M., and Benjamin Siegel. "At War in Iraq and Afghanistan: Children in U.S. Military Families." *Ambulatory Pediatrics* 7 (2007) 1–2.

Clinebell, Howard J., Jr. "The Local Church's Contributions to Positive Mental Health." In *Community Mental Health: The Role of Church and Temple*, edited by Howard J. Clinebell, Jr., 46–56. Nashville: Abingdon, 1970.

Congressional Budget Office. "The Effects of Reserve Call-Ups on Civilian Employers." Online: http://www.cbo.gov/publication/16506.

Crary, David. "As Wars Lengthen, Toll on Military Families Mounts." *The Huffington Post*, July 19, 2008. Online: http://www.huffingtonpost.com/huff-wires/20080719/ military-scarred-families/.

Debbink, Dirk J. "Welcome Aboard." *The Navy Reservist: 2010 Almanac*. Online: https:// www.navyreserve.navy.mil/Publications/TNR/Almanac/TNRAlmanac2010.pdf.

Defense Science Board Task Force. "Deployment of Members of the National Guard and Reserve in the Global War on Terrorism." Office of the Under Secretary of Defense for Acquisition, Technology, and Logistics, 2007. Online: http://www.acq.osd.mil/ dsb/reports/ADA478163.pdf.

DeVelder, John. "The Effects of War on Pastoral Care and Counseling." *Pastoral Report: The Newsletter of the College of Pastoral Supervision and Psychotherapy*, December 28, 2006. Online: http://www.pastoralreport.com/the_archives/2006/12/the_ effects_of.html.

"DoD Issues Medical Advisory on Leishmaniasis; Blood Donations Halted." Online: www. publichealth.va.gov/docs/oefoif/OIF_OEF_Review_Dec_2003.pdf.

Doyle, Thomas P. "The Marriages of Military Personnel: A Special Question." *Military Chaplains' Review*, Winter 1988, 29–39.

Dreher, Rod. "Ministers of War: The Amazing Chaplaincy of the U.S. Military." *National Review*, March 10, 2003. Online: http://www.orthodoxytoday.org/articles4/ DreherChaplains.php.

Duckett, Paul. "Globalised Violence, Community Psychology and the Bombing and Occupation of Afghanistan and Iraq." *Journal of Community and Applied Social Psychology* 15 (2005) 414–23.

Ender, Morten G. "Voices from the Backseat: Demands of Growing Up in Military Families." In *Military Life: The Psychology of Serving in Peace and Combat*, edited by Thomas W. Britt, Carl A. Castro, and Amy B. Adler, 3:138–66. Westport, CT: Praeger Security International, 2006.

Feidler, Bob. DoD/VA Healthcare Symposium. "Part I: Total Force Care." Paper presented at a conference sponsored by the Defense Education Forum, Reserve Officers Association, Washington, DC, November 19, 2008. Online: http://www.roa.org/site/ DocServer/20090428_FINALREPORTTWOHCPROGRAMS.pdf?docID=15601. html.

———. DoD/VA Healthcare Symposium. "Part II: Mental Healthcare Delivery to the Armed Forces Reserve Officer." Paper presented at a conference sponsored by Defense Education Forum, Reserve Officers Association, Washington, DC, March 23, 2009. Online: http://www.roa.org/site/DocServer/20090428_ FINALREPORTTWOHCPROGRAMS.pdf?docID=15601.html.

Feuerherd, Joe. "Military Chaplains see Conflict Differently." *National Catholic Reporter,* April 4, 2003, 5.

Ford, Daniel. "B-36: Bomber at the Crossroads." *Air and Space Magazine,* April 1, 1996. Online: http://www.airspacemag.com/history-of-flight/B-36-Bomber-at-the-Crossroads.html?c=y&page=1.

Gibbs, Nancy. "Sexual Assaults on Female Soldiers: Don't Ask, Don't Tell." *Time,* March 8, 2010. Online: http://www.time.com/time/magazine/article/0,9171,1968110,00. html.

Goldstein, David. "Suicides Increase a Mystery, Guard and Reserve: The Military Has Improved Mental Health Programs, but the Problem Persists." *Press-Enterprise* [Riverside, CA], July 25, 2010, C2.

Gorman, Gregory H., Matilde Eide, and Elizabeth Hisle-Gorman. "Wartime Military Deployment and Increased Pediatric Mental and Behavioral Health Complaints." Online: http://pediatrics.aappublications.org/content/126/6/1058.full.

Graham, Bradley. "General Says Army Reserve Is Becoming a Broken Force." *The Washington Post,* January 6, 2005.

Gravois, John. "Escape from Iraq." *The Chronicle of Higher Education,* February 23, 2007, A10.

Greider, Kathleen. "Nonviolent Conflicts and Cultural Differences: Essentials for Practicing Peace." In *Choosing Peace through Daily Practices,* edited by Ellen Ott Marshall, 129–57. Cleveland: Pilgrim, 2005.

Griffith, James. "The Army Reserve Soldier in Operation Desert Storm: Perceptions of Being Prepared for Mobilization, Deployment, and Combat." *Armed Forces and Society* 21 (1995) 195–215.

Iasiello, Louis V. "The Chaplain as Noncombatant Serving Combatants." In *Voices of Chaplaincy,* edited by David E. White. Arlington, VA: Military Chaplains Association, 2002.

Immortal Chaplains Foundation. "The Story of the Four Immortal Chaplains." Online: http://www.immortalchaplains.org/Story/story.htm.

Isikoff, Michael. "Lawsuit Claims Pentagon Turned Blind Eye to Military Rape Victims." Online: http://www.msnbc.msn.com/id/41598622/ns/us_news-life/t/lawsuit-claims-pentagon-turned-blind-eye-military-rape-victims/.

Jakupcak, Matthew, et al. "Anger, Hostility, and Subthreshold PTSD." *Journal of Traumatic Stress* 20 (2007) 945–54.

Jervis, Rick. "Chaplains: We Are Traumatized, Too." *USA Today,* December 16, 2009. Reprinted in *NCMAF/ECVAC Newsletter: News and Resources for Military and Veterans Affairs Endorsers and Chaplains,* Winter 2009, 3.

Johnston, Douglas M. "The U.S. Military Chaplaincy: Redirecting A Critical Asset." *Review of Faith and International Affairs* 7 (2009) 25–32.

"Joint Chief of Staff Chairman: TRICARE Tops Guards, Reserve Families' Concerns." Association of the United States Army. Online: http://www.ausa.org.news/2010/ Pages /Slug1October.aspx.

Jones, Warren A. "The A-B-C Method of Crisis Management." *Mental Hygiene* 52 (1968) 87–89.

Jonsson, Patrik. "Troubled Soldiers Turn to Chaplains for Help." *Christian Science Monitor*, March 8, 2006. Online: http://www.csmonitor.com/2006/0308/p01s03-usmi.html.

Joyner, Bo. "Deployment Support: Command Strives for Continuous Improvements in Helping Reservists and Their Families Deal with Separations." *Citizen Airman*, August 2008, 8.

Juarez-Palma, Nils. "Pastoral Care to Hispanic Military Families." *Military Chaplains' Review*, Summer 1992, 9–18.

Judis, John. "An American Suicide: What War Did to Jeffrey Lucey." Online: http://www.carnegieendowment.org/2007/08/06/american-suicide-what-war-did-to-jeffrey-lucey/d46.

Kane, Tim. "Who Are the Recruits? The Demographic Characteristics of U.S. Military Enlistment, 2003–2005." Online: http://www.heritage.org/research/reports/2006/10/who-are-the-recruits-the-demographic-characteristics-of-us-military-enlistment-2003-2005.

———. "Who Bears the Burden? Demographic Characteristics of U.S. Military Recruits Before and After 9/11." Online: http://www.heritage.org/research/reports/2005/11/who-bears-the-burden-demographic-characteristics-of-us-military-recruits-before-and-after-9-11.

Kim, Stephen K. "Pastoral Care to Asian-American Families." *Military Chaplains' Review*, Summer 1992, 19–28.

Klingner, Donald, and L. R. Jones. "Learning from the Philippine Occupation: Nation-Building and Institutional Development in Iraq and Other High Security Risk Nations." *Public Administration and Development* 25 (2005) 145–56.

Kozaryn, Linda D. "Muslim Troops Highlight Nation's Diversity." American Forces Information Services, January 26, 1999. Online: http://www.defenselink.mil/news/Jan1999/n01261999_9901261.html.

Lakhani, Hyder, and Stephen S. Fugita. "Reserve/Guard Retention: Moonlighting or Patriotism?" *Military Psychology* 5 (1993) 123.

Landrum, Cecile S. "The Changing Military Family: An Increased Role for the Chaplain." Occasional Papers No. 41. Nashville: United Methodist Board of Higher Education and Ministry, 1982.

Lapp, Cheryl Ann, et al. "Stress and Coping on the Home Front: Guard and Reserve Spouses Searching for a New Normal." *Journal of Family Nursing* 16 (2010) 45–67.

Lartey, Emmanuel. "Practical Theology as a Theological Form." In *The Blackwell Reader in Pastoral and Practical Theology*, edited by James Woodward and Stephen Pattison, 128–34. Oxford: Blackwell, 2000.

Leroe, Robert G. "The Effects of Hardship Tours on Children." *Military Chaplains' Review*, Winter 1988, 49–55.

Levin, Diane E., and Carol Iskols Daynard. "The 'SOFAR' Guide for Helping Children and Youth Cope with the Deployment of a Parent in the Military Reserves." SOFAR Project Guide. Psychoanalytic Couple and Family Institute of New England, 2005. Online: http://www.sofarusa.org/downleads/sofar_children_pamphlet.pdf.

Lomsky-Feder, Edna, Nir Gazit, and Eyal Ben-Ari. "Reserve Soldiers as Transmigrants: Moving between the Civilian and the Military Worlds." *Armed Forces and Society* 34 (2008) 593–614.

Lopez, Steve. "A Combat Veteran's Struggle of the Soul." *Los Angeles Times*, February 13, 2011, A2.

Loveland, Anne C. "From Morale Builders to Moral Advocates: U.S. Army Chaplains in the Second Half of the Twentieth Century." In *The Sword of the Lord: Military Chaplains from the First to the Twenty-First Century*, edited by Doris L. Bergen, 233–50. Notre Dame: University of Notre Dame Press, 2004.

McCoy, Shane T. "Service in the Sand: Keeping Warriors in the War." *All Hands*, July 2005. Online: http://findarticles.com/p/articles/mi_m0IBQ/is_1059/ai_n15674243/.

McGarry, Brendan. "Two Careers, Two Jobs: Reservists Juggle Heavier Load Since 9/11." *Air Force Times*, May 18, 2009, 26.

Mendenhall, Marty. "Chaplains in Mental Health: Healing the Spiritual Wounds of War." Online: http://www.americanpsychotherapy.me/2010/08/chaplains-in-mental-health-healing-the-spiritual-wounds-of-war/, August 9, 2010, 4.

Miles, Donna. "Obama Pledges Support for Fort Hood Community." American Forces Press Service. Online: http://preview.defenselink.mil/news/newsarticle. aspx?id=56556&456556=20091105.

Miller, Rodney K. "In Two Worlds: The Pastoral Care of Reserve Component Soldiers: The Civilian Job and the Military Mission." *Military Chaplains' Review*, Winter 1991, 11–19.

Molitor, Nancy, Ronald Palomares, and Morgan Sammons. "Resilience in a Time of War: Homecoming." American Psychological Association, 2008. Online: http://www.apa. org/helpcenter/homecoming.aspx.

National Guard Family Program. "Family Readiness: Step 4, Pre-deployment." Online: http://www.jointservicessupport.org/FP/step4.aspx.

National Military Family Association. "Report on the Cycles of Deployment: An Analysis of Survey Responses from April through September, 2005." Online: http://www. nmfa.org/site/DocServer/NMFACyclesofDeployment9.pdf?docID=54501.html.

———. "Ten Things Military Teens Want You to Know." Online: http://www. militaryfamily.org/publications/teen-toolkit/.

"No Thanks for Your Service: Guardmembers and Reservists Deserve Relief." *Military Officer*, February 2010, 36.

Olivarez, Isaac. "Pastoring the Air Force's 'Pastors': Interview with Cecil Richardson." *Pentecostal Evangel*, June 27, 2004.

O'Malley, Colleen J., et al. "Children's Reported Communication with Their Parents about War." *Journal of Family Issues* 28 (2007) 1639–662.

Parker, Ned, and Raheem Salman. "A Christian Priest Faces Grim New Year in Iraq." *Los Angeles Times*, January 1, 2011. Online: http://articles.latimes.com/2011/jan/01/ world/la-fg-iraq-priest-20110101.

Petraeus, David H. "Learning Counterinsurgency: Observations from Soldiering in Iraq." *Military Review*, January-February 2006.

Phillips, Robert. "The Military Chaplain in Time of War: Contours and Content of Ministry." *Quarterly Review* 24 (2004) 47–58.

Powers, Rod. "Deployment Rates: Iraq and Afghanistan from September 11, 2001 to 31 October 2004." Online: http://usmilitary.about.com/od/terrorism/a/ deploymentrates.htm.

Rohall, David E., Morten G. Ender, and Michael D. Matthews. "The Effects of Military Affliation, Gender, and Political Ideology on Attitudes." *Armed Forces and Society* 33 (2006) 59–77.

Roswell, Robert. "Under Secretary for Health Information Letter: Clinical Reminder Regarding Veterans of the Recent Conflicts in Afghanistan and Iraq." Washington, DC: U. S. Department of Veterans Affairs, February 2004.

Saltzman, Jonathan. "Family Settles with U.S. in Marine Suicide." *The Boston Globe*, January 16, 2009. Online: http://www.boston.com/news/local/massachusetts/articles/2009/01/16/family_settles_with_us_in_marine_suicide/.

Segal, David R., and Mady Wechsler Segal. "America's Military Population." *Population Bulletin*, Population Reference Bureau, December 2004.

————. "U.S. Military's Reliance on the Reserves." Population Reference Bureau, 2005. Online: http:www.prb.org/Articles/2005/USMilitarysRelianceontheReserves.aspx?p=1.

Segal, Mady Wechsler, and David R. Segal. "Latinos Claim Larger Share of U.S. Military Personnel." Population Reference Bureau, October 2007.

Shane, Scott. "A Flood of Troubled Soldiers Is in the Offing, Experts Predict." *The New York Times*, December 16, 2004. Online: http://www.nytimes.com/2004/12/16/national/16stress.html.

Shattuck, Gardiner H., Jr. "Faith, Morale, and the Army Chaplain in the American Civil War." In *The Sword of the Lord: Military Chaplains from the First to the Twenty-First Century*, edited by Doris L. Bergen, 105–24. Notre Dame: University of Notre Dame Press, 2004.

Sorley, Lewis. "Creighton Abrams and Active-Reserve Integration in Wartime." *PARAMETERS: US Army War College Quarterly* 21 (1991) 35–50.

Soucy, Jon. "Army, Air Guard Maintain End Strength." National Guard Bureau. Online: http://www.ng.mil/news/archives/2010/07/072910-Strenth.aspx, 1.

Starling, I. C., Jr. "Military Service and Military Chaplaincy." In *Dictionary of Pastoral Care and Counseling*, edited by Rodney J. Hunter, 726–27. Nashville: Abingdon, 1990.

Strumwasser, Brad. "The Effects of Deployment on the Family: A Professional and Personal Account." *Los Angeles Psychologist* 23 (2009) 16–17.

Stultz, Jack C., and Michael D. Schultz. "The United States Army Reserve 2010 Posture Statement: A Positive Investment for America." U.S. Army Reserve, March 2010. Online: http://www.usar.army.mil/arweb/mission/ARPS2010/Pages/ARPShomepage.aspx.

Thomasson, Dan K. "Deployed Troops Should Be Protected from Foreclosure." *San Francisco Examiner*, February 2, 2011. Online: http://www.sfexaminer.com/opinion/op-eds/2011/02/deployed-troops-should-be-protected-foreclosure.

Thompson, Richard D. "Homecoming: A Period of Adjustment." *Military Chaplains' Review*, Winter 1991, 21–29.

Townsend, James E. "Families in Blue: A Ministry Model." Occasional Papers No. 42. Nashville: United Methodist Board of Higher Education and Ministry, 1982.

Uniformed Services University of the Health Sciences. "Courage to Care: Reintegration Roadmap." Online: http://www.cstsonline.org/courage-to-care-reintegration-roadmap/.

U.S. Air Force. Chaplain Service Institute. "Staying Together while Apart." [Maxwell AFB] Montgomery, AL: Resource Division, January 1997.

U.S. Air Force Reserve. "AFR 2012: Command Makes It Easier for Reservists to Volunteer, Mobilize, Deploy." *Citizen Airman*, August 2010, 16.

————. "Air Force Command—Chaplain Candidate." Online: http://www.afrc.af.mil/library/chaplain/howtojoin/candidate/index.asp.

————. "U.S. Air Force Reserve SNAPSHOT." Online: http://www.afrc.af.mil/shared/media/document/AFD-060712-018.pdf.

————. "Who We Are." Online: http://afreserve.com/?:Who We Are.

U.S. Army Reserve. "History." Online: http://www.usar.army.mil/ourstory/History/Pages/Publications.aspx.

U.S. Coast Guard. "History of the Coast Guard Reserve." Online: http://www.uscg.mil/history/articles/CG_Reserve_History.asp.

U.S. Congress. House Committee on Armed Services. Subcommittee on Military Personnel. "Active Army, Army National Guard, and Army Reserve Recruiting and Retention Programs: Hearing." House of Representatives, 110th Congress, 1st Session, August 1, 2007. Washington, DC: U.S. GPO, 2008.

U.S. Department of Defense. *Guard and Reserve Family Readiness for the Twenty-First Century*. Reserve Component Common Personnel Data System: 1998, DD-RA Year End Report. Online: http://www.virtualarmory.com/family/familyreadiness.pdf.

————. Office of Defense Mobilization Advisory Committee on Production Equipment. "Production Capacity: A Military Reserve Report to the Director of Defense Mobilization." Washington, DC: GPO, 1953.

————. Office of the Assistant Secretary of Defense for Reserve Affairs. "Managing the Reserve Components as an Operational Force." Washington, DC: 2008.

————. Office of the Deputy Under Secretary of Defense. "Demographics 2008: Profile of the Military Community." http://cs.mhf.dod.mil/content/dav/mhf/QOL-Library/Project%20Documents/MilitaryHOMEFRONT/Reports/2008%20Demographics.pdf.

————. Reserve Component Common Personnel Data System: 1998 DD-RA Year End Report. "Guard and Reserve Family Readiness for the Twenty-First Century."

————. Reserve Forces Policy Board. "Annual Report." Washington, DC: Office of the Secretary of Defense, 2004.

U. S. Department of the Navy. "FY 04 Profile of Navy." September 15, 2004. Online: http://www.armyg1.army.mil/hr/docs/.../fy04%20navy%20profile.pdf.

U.S. Department of Veterans Affairs. National Center for Post-Traumatic Stress Disorder and Walter Reed Hospital. "Iraq War Clinician Guide." 2nd ed. June 2004.

————. *Operations Enduring Freedom/ Iraqi Freedom Review*, October 2007.

U.S. Marine Corps. Community Services. "A Young and Vigorous Force." December 2008. Online: http://www.usmc_mccs.org/aboutmccs/.../Demographics%20Update Dec2008, pdf.

U.S. Navy Reserve. "Navy Reserve History." Online: http://www.navyreserve.com/about/history/.

U.S. Selective Service System. "Draft Policy Revision." Online: http://www.sss.gov/viet.htm.

U.S. Under Secretary for Health. Information Letter. "Guidance for the Diagnosis and Treatment of Leishmania Infection." October 6, 2004. Online: http://1nightingale.websitetoolbox.com/post?id=1608608.

Vaughn, Clyde A. "Message from the Director of Army National Guard: National Guard Posture Statement 2010, America's Indispensable Force." Online: http://www.ng.mil/features/ngps/2010-nyps.pdf.

Veterans for America. "The American Veterans and Service Members Survival Guide." Online: http://www.veteransforamerica.org/survival-guide.

Volf, Miroslav. "Agents of Peace in Theaters of War: Rethinking the Role of Military Chaplains." *Review of Faith and International Affairs* 7 (2009) 33–41.

Wilson, Elaine. "Balancing Act Strains Reservists." American Forces Press Service, *The BEACON*, January 22, 2010, 9.

Zellman, Gail L., et al. "Meeting Family and Military Needs through Military Child Care." *Armed Forces and Society* 35 (2009) 437–59.

Zoroya, Gregg. "Witnesses Say Reservist was a Hero at Hood." *USA Today*, November 25, 2009. Online: http://www.armytimes.com/news/2009/11/gns_hero_112509/.

BOOKS

Adams, George. *Chaplains as Liaisons with Religious Leaders: Lessons from Iraq and Afghanistan*. Washington, DC: United States Institute of Peace, 2006.

Andrews, Dale P. *Practical Theology for Black Churches: Bridging Black Theology and African American Folk Religion*. Louisville: Westminster John Knox, 2002.

Armstrong, Keith, Suzanne Best, and Paula Domenici. *Courage after Fire: Coping Strategies for Troops Returning from Iraq and Afghanistan and Their Families*. Berkeley: Ulysses, 2005.

Arnove, Anthony. *Iraq: The Logic of Withdrawal*. New York: New Press, 2006.

Benhoff, David A., and Anthony Zinn. *Among the People: U.S. Marines in Iraq*. Quantico, VA: Marine Corps University, 2008.

Benimoff, Roger, with Eve Conant. *Faith under Fire: An Army Chaplain's Memoir*. New York: Crown, 2009.

Bergsma, Herbert L. *Chaplains with Marines in Vietnam, 1962–1971*. Washington, DC: History and Museums Division, Headquarters, U.S. Marine Corps, 1985.

Berkley, James D., editor. *Leadership Handbook of Outreach and Care*. Grand Rapids: Baker, 1994.

Binkin, Martin. *U.S. Reserve Forces: The Problem of the Weekend Warrior*. Washington, D.C.: Brookings Institution, 1974.

Bouillon, Markus E., David M. Malone, and Ben Rowswell, editors. *Iraq: Preventing a New Generation of Conflict*. Boulder, CO: Lynne Rienner, 2007.

Britt, Thomas W., Carl A. Castro, and Amy B. Adler, editors. *Military Life: The Psychology of Serving in Peace and Combat*. 4 vols. Westport, CT: Praeger Security International, 2006.

Brogan, Edward T. *The Chaplain as Advocate*. Ft. Belvoir, VA: Defense Technical Information Center, 1987.

Brown, Davis. *The Sword, the Cross, and the Eagle: The American Christian Just War Tradition*. Lanham, MD: Rowman & Littlefield, 2008.

Browning, Don S. *A Fundamental Practical Theology: Descriptive and Strategic Proposals*. Minneapolis: Fortress, 1991.

Byman, Daniel, and Kenneth M. Pollack. *Things Fall Apart: Containing the Spillover from an Iraqi Civil War*. Washington, DC: Brookings Institution Press, 2007.

Carroll, Andrew. *Grace Under Fire: Letters of Faith in Times of War*. Colorado Springs, CO: Waterbrook, 2007.

Cash, Carey H. *A Table in the Presence*. Nashville: W Publishing Group, 2004.

Castro, Carl Andrew, Amy B. Adler, and Thomas W. Britt, eds. *The Military Family: The Psychology of Serving in Peace and Combat*. Vol. 3. Westport, CT: Praeger, 2006.

Clinebell, Howard J., Jr. *Basic Types of Pastoral Care and Counseling: Resources for the Ministry of Healing and* Growth. Rev. ed. Nashville: Abingdon, 1984.

———. "Global Peacemaking and Wholeness: Developing Justice-Based Theological, Psychological, and Spiritual Resources: Findings of Theory-Generating Conference." Sponsored by the Institute for Religion and Wholeness, May 17–19, 1984. Claremont School of Theology, 1984.

———. *The Mental Health Ministry of the Local Church*. Nashville: Abingdon, 1972.

———. *Well Being: A Personal Plan for Exploring and Enriching the Seven Dimensions of Life: Mind, Body, Spirit, Love, Work, Play, the Earth*. San Francisco: HarperSanFrancisco, 1992.

Drury, Clifford Merrill. *The History of the Chaplain Corps, United States Navy*. Vol. 6, *During the Korean War, 27 June 1950–27 June 1954*. Washington, DC: GPO, 1960.

Edgren, James A. "Military Chaplains." In *Leadership Handbook of Outreach and Care*, edited by James D. Berkley, 445–53. Grand Rapids: Baker Books, 1994.

Elshtain, Jean Bethke. *Just War against Terror: The Burden of American Power in a Violent World*. New York: Basic Books, 2003.

Fawn, Rick, and Raymond Hinnebusch, editors. *The Iraq War: Causes and Consequences*. Boulder, CO: Lynne Rienner, 2006.

Feldman, Shai, editor. *After the War in Iraq: Defending the New Strategic Balance*. Brighton, UK: Sussex Academic, 2003.

Fettweis, Christopher J. *Losing Hurts Twice as Bad: The Four Stages to Moving Beyond Iraq*. New York: Norton, 2008.

Galbraith, Peter W. *Unintended Consequences: How War in Iraq Strengthened America's Enemies*. New York: Simon & Schuster, 2008.

Greider, Kathleen J. *Much Madness Is Divinest Sense: Wisdom in Memoirs of Soul-Suffering*. Cleveland: Pilgrim, 2007.

———. *Reckoning with Aggression: Theology, Violence, and Vitality*. Louisville: Westminster John Knox, 1997.

Gross, Charles Joseph. *The Air National Guard and the American Military Tradition: Militiaman, Volunteer, and Professional*. Washington, DC: National GuardBureau, 1995.

Gushwa, Robert L. *The Best and Worst of Times: The United States Army Chaplaincy, 1920–1945*. Washington, DC: Office of the Chief of Chaplains, Department of the Army, 1977.

Hadley, Donald W., and Gerald T. Richards. *Ministry with the Military: A Guide for Churches and Chaplains*. Grand Rapids: Baker, 1992.

Harris, Thomas A. *Counseling the Serviceman and His Family*. Englewood Cliffs, NJ: Prentice-Hall, 1964.

Heitink, Gerben. *Practical Theology: History, Theory, Action Domains; Manual for Practical Theology*. Translated by Reinder Bruinsma. Grand Rapids: Eerdmans, 1999.

Honeywell, Roy J. *Chaplains of the United States Army*. Washington, DC: Office of the Chief of Chaplains, Department of the Army, 1958.

Horton, Anthony W. *Finding Faith in the Desert: An LDS Military Chaplain Finds Light and Hope among the U.S. Soldiers and Iraqi People amidst the Challenges of Operation Iraqi Freedom*. Provo, UT: Spring Creek, 2004.

Hosek, James R., Jennifer Kavanagh, and Laura L. Miller. *How Deployments Affect Service Members*. Santa Monica, CA: Rand Corporation, 2006.

Bibliography

Hosmer, Stephen T. *Why the Iraqi Resistance to the Coalition Invasion Was So Weak*. Santa Monica, CA: Rand Corporation, 2007.

Hunter, Rodney J., editor. *Dictionary of Pastoral Care and Counseling*. Nashville: Abingdon, 1990.

Janis, Irving L. *Air War and Emotional Stress: Psychological Studies of Bombing and Civilian Defense*. New York: McGraw-Hill, 1951.

Jorgensen, Daniel B. *Air Force Chaplains, 1947–1960*. Washington, DC: Office of the Chief of Air Force Chaplains, 1961.

———. *The Service of Chaplains to Army Air Units, 1917–1946*. Washington, DC: Office of the Chief of Air Force Chaplains, 1961.

Kaslow, Florence W., editor. *The Military Family in Peace and War*. New York: Springer, 1993.

Kaslow, Florence W., and Richard I. Ridenour, editors. *The Military Family: Dynamics and Treatment*. New York: Guilford, 1984.

Kennedy, Carrie H., and Eric A. Zillmer, editors. *Military Psychology: Clinical and Operational Applications*. New York: Guilford, 2006.

Kittleson, Lance. *Meditations from Iraq: A Chaplain's Ministry in the Middle East, 2003–2004*. Lima, OH: CSS, 2005.

Lebacqz, Karen, and Joseph D. Driskill. *Ethics and Spiritual Care: A Guide for Pastors and Spiritual Directors*. Nashville: Abingdon, 2000.

Leinwand, Gerald, and Steven McLaine, comps. *The Draft*. New York: Washington Square, 1970.

Marrero, Emilio. *A Quiet Reality: A Chaplain's Journey into Babylon, Iraq with the 1st Marine Expeditionary Force*. Lima, OH: Faith Walk, 2009.

Martin, James A., Leora N. Rosen, and Linette R. Sparacino, editors. *The Military Family: A Practice Guide for Human Service Providers*. Westport, CT: Praeger, 2000.

Matsakis, Aphrodite. *Back from the Front: Combat Trauma, Love, and the Family*. Baltimore: Sidran Institute Press, 2007.

McBride, J. LeBron. *Spiritual Crisis: Surviving Trauma to the Soul*. New York: Haworth Pastoral Press, 1998.

McCoy, William. *Under Orders: A Spiritual Handbook for Military Personnel*. Ozark, AL: ACW, 2005.

Moore, Thomas. *Care of the Soul: A Guide for Cultivating Depth and Sacredness in Everyday Life*. New York: HarperCollins, 1992.

Musheno, Michael C., and Susan M. Ross. *Deployed: How Reservists Bear the Burden of Iraq*. Ann Arbor: University of Michigan Press, 2008.

Newby, Claude D. *It Took Heroes: A Cavalry Chaplain's Memoir of Vietnam*. New York: Ballantine, 1998.

Paget, Naomi K., and Janet R. McCormack. *The Work of the Chaplain*. Valley Forge, PA: Judson, 2006.

Pattison, Stephen. *The Challenge of Practical Theology: Selected Essays*. London: Jessica Kingsley, 2007.

Paulson, Daryl S., and Stanley Krippner. *Haunted by Combat: Understanding PTSD in War Veterans Including Women, Reservists, and Those Coming Back from Iraq*. Westport, CT: Praeger Security International, 2007.

Pavlicin, Karen M. *Surviving Deployment: A Guide for Military Families*. St. Paul, MN: Elva Resa, 2003.

Plekenpol, Chris. *Faith in the Fog of War*. Sisters, OR: Multnomah, 2006.

Rogers, Dalene C. Fuller. *Pastoral Care for Post-Traumatic Stress Disorder: Healing the Shattered Soul.* New York: Haworth Pastoral Press, 2002.

Rosenfeld, Susan, and Charles J. Gross. *Air National Guard at Sixty: A History.* Arlington, VA: Air National Guard, 2007.

Sauds, Nulvin S. *Chaplains' Spiritual Ministry for All Faiths in War Emergency.* N.p., 19–.

Schmidt, Jeremy. *Melancholy and the Care of the Soul: Religion, Moral Philosophy and Madness in Early Modern England.* Aldershot, UK: Ashgate, 2007.

Sifry, Micah L., and Christopher Cerf. *The Iraq War Reader: History, Documents, Opinions.* New York: Simon & Schuster, 2003.

Silver, Anne Winehell. *Trustworthy Connections: Interpersonal Issues in Spiritual Direction.* Cambridge: Cowley, 2003.

Smith, Robert London, Jr. *From Strength to Strength: Shaping a Black Practical Theology for the Twenty-First Century.* New York: Peter Lang, 2007.

Snow, Donald M. *What after Iraq?* New York: Pearson/Longman, 2009.

Steele, David A. *Reconciliation Strategies in Iraq.* Washington, DC: U.S. Institute of Peace, 2008.

Stone, Howard W. *Brief Pastoral Counseling: Short-Term Approach and Strategies.* Minneapolis: Fortress, 1994.

———. *The Caring Church: A Guide for Lay Pastoral Care.* San Francisco: Harper & Row, 1983.

Stover, Earl F. *Up from Handymen: The United States Army Chaplaincy, 1865–1920.* Washington, DC: Office of the Chief of Chaplains, Department of the Army, 1977.

Tanielian, Terri, and Lisa Jaycox. *Invisible Wounds of War: Psychological and Cognitive Injuries, Their Consequences, and Services to Assist Recovery.* Santa Monica, CA: Rand Corporation, 2008.

Thomas, James Samuel. *Military Chaplaincy: A Study of the Participation of the United Methodist Church in the Present System of Military Chaplaincy.* Arlington, VA: Division of Chaplains and Related Ministries, Board of Higher Education and Ministry, The United Methodist Church, 1979.

Thompson, David A., and Darlene Wetterstrom. *Beyond the Yellow Ribbon: Ministering to Returning Combat Veterans.* Nashville: Abingdon, 2009.

United Methodist Church (U.S.). *The United Methodist Book of Worship.* Nashville: Abingdon, 1992.

U.S. Air Force. Chaplain Service Resource Board. *Pastoral Ministry Team Handbook: Providing the Keys to Effective Readiness Training and Ministry.* [Maxwell AFB] Montgomery, AL: Resource Board, 1992.

U.S. General Accounting Office. *Reserve Forces: Proposals to Expand Call-Up Authorities Should Include Numerical Limitations.* Washington, DC: GPO, 1997.

U. S. Marine Corps. Division of Reserve. *The Marine Corps Reserve: A History.* Washington, DC: GPO, 1996.

Weatherhead, Leslie D. *Thinking Aloud in War-Time.* New York: Abingdon, 1940.

Weiss, Thomas George. *Military-Civilian Interactions: Intervening in Humanitarian Crisis.* Lanham, MD: Rowman & Littlefield, 1999.

Westling, Lester Leon. *When Johnny/Joanie Comes Marching Home: Reuniting Military Families Following Deployment.* Gainesville, GA: Praxis, 2005.

Wismer, Frank E., III. *War in the Garden of Eden: A Military Chaplain's Memoir from Baghdad.* New York: Seabury, 2008.

Woodward, James, and Stephen Pattison, editors. *The Blackwell Reader in Pastoral and Practical Theology.* Oxford: Blackwell, 2000.

PAPERS, THESES, AND DISSERTATIONS/UNPUBLISHED WORKS

Adams, Richard L. "A Systems Approach to Pastoral Care in the Military Community." DMin project, Claremont School of Theology, 1985.

Arauco, Oscar T. "A Chaplain's Preparation for Combat: A Primer on How to Prepare for Combat Ministry." MA thesis, Army Command and General Staff College, 2005.

Coffey, Gary Dale. "Spiritual Survival during Deployment: Supporting the Soldier in a Foreign Environment." DMin thesis, Pittsburgh Theological Seminary, 2003.

Dugal, Michael W. "Affirming the Soldier's Spirit through Intentional Dialogue." In *Strategy Research Project.* Carlisle Barracks, PA: U.S. Army War College, 2009.

Ginsberg, Daniel B. Review of the Defense Authorization Request for Fiscal Year 2011 and the Future Years Defense Program. Online: http://armed-services.senate.gov/statemnt/2010/03%20March/Ginsberg%2003-10-10.pdf).

Gray, Gerald R. "A Model of Ministry for the United States Navy Chaplain Corps for Effectively Meeting the Needs of Generation Xers and Millennium Generation Sailors and Marines." DMin thesis, Columbia Theological Seminary, 2003.

Hart, Robert. "The Differing Views of Just War from the Sunni and Shiite Muslim Traditions and Moral Relevance for United States Military Forces Operating with Them." MA thesis, Southern Baptist Theological Seminary, 2008.

Hoge, Charles, W., Carl A. Castro, and Karen M. Eaton. "Impact of Combat Duty in Iraq and Afghanistan on Family Functioning: Findings from the Walter Reed Army Institute of Research Land Combat Study." Paper submitted for Human Factors and Medicine Panel Symposium (HFM-134) on Human Dimensions in Military Operations, Meetings Proceedings, NATO Research and Technology Organization, 2006.

Kurashina, Yuko, Meyer Kestenbaum, and David R. Segal. "The Military Participation Ratio (MPR) Update: Mobilization of Non-Active Duty Personnel." Paper presented at the annual meetings of the American Sociological Association, Chicago, August 2004.

Muehler, Craig G. "The Role of the Navy Core Values in Christian Counseling: An Exploration in Integration for the Navy Chaplain." MA thesis, Trinity Evangelical Divinity School, 2001.

O'Connor, Jillian Bailey. "Why They Fight: Veterans, Civilians and the Divergent Experience of War." MA thesis, Claremont Graduate University, 2007.

Vickers, Robert C. "The Military Chaplaincy: A Study in Role Conflict." PhD diss., Vanderbilt University, 1984.